Read It Again!

MULTICULTURAL • GRADES 1-3

Multicultural Books for the Primary Grades

Liz Rothlein, Ed. D.
Terri Christman Wild, M. Ed.

Illustrated by Toni Summers

GoodYearBooks
An Imprint of ScottForesman
A Division of HarperCollins Publisher

To Fritz and Edith Lang, my gracious hosts in Switzerland. Thank you for allowing me the opportunity to stay in your charming and petite Alpine chalet, which is nestled in a panorama of majestic mountain views. My stay there was the inspiration for this book.
—LR

To Ash Rothlein, my stepfather and friend, who continually sees the good in all people.
—TCW

Many individuals "touched" this book with their expertise. We recognize their contributions and feel their support, and we are grateful to all of you: Roberta Dempsey, for seeing us through from start to finish; Linda Western, for the excellent reviewing and editing of our manuscript; Violet Harris, for her review of the manuscript; and Mike Hurley and Beverly Mayo, for their care and understanding during the preparation of this manuscript.

Good Year Books
are available for most basic curriculum subjects plus many enrichment areas. For more Good Year Books, contact your local bookseller or educational dealer. For a complete catalog with information about other Good Year Books, please write:

Good Year Books
Scott, Foresman and Company
1900 East Lake Avenue
Glenview, IL 60025

Cover illustration by Yoshi Miyake.
Design by Street Level Studio.
Copyright © 1993 Liz Rothlein and Terri Christman Wild.
All Rights Reserved.
Printed in the United States of America.

ISBN 0-673-36064-4

2 3 4 5 6 7 8 9 10 – ER – 02 01 00 99 98 97 96 95 94

CONTENTS

Introduction

Setting the Stage

People of Asian Roots and Their Traditions

People of African Roots and Their Traditions

Hispanic Peoples and Their Traditions

Native Americans and Their Legacy

Appendix

INTRODUCTION

Our country is becoming increasingly diverse. The 1990 U.S. Census reveals that America has the largest foreign-born population in its history. Nationally, 19.7 million persons, or just under 8 percent of the population, were born in another country. Many of these immigrants are Asians or Hispanics. Nearly 32 million persons speak a language other than English at home, and more than 40 percent of those do not speak English very well. According to Felicity Barringer (1991), "The racial complexion of the American population changed more dramatically in the past decade than at any time in the 20th century, with nearly one in every four Americans (now) having African, Asian, Hispanic, or American Indian ancestry."

The question remains, "How can a nation such as the United States embrace the diversity of so many cultures?" Richard A. Shweder (1991), in his review of Carl Degler's book *In Search of Human Nature,* comments on our struggle to be "comfortable with diversity":

> As our liberal democracy stands poised at the start of another round of debates about pluralism, multiculturalism, and group differences, it is incumbent upon us to understand why such debates are so difficult, painful, threatening . . . and why, and on what terms, we must have them nonetheless. (pp. 1, 30, 31, 35)

These debates occur because people often have difficulties in understanding and accepting our culturally diverse and complex society; they also stem from issues of who has power in our society and the privileges that accrue from possessing that power. We, as educators and parents, must prepare our children to live and work harmoniously and productively in an increasingly multicultural society. If we provide resources that allow for an exploration and understanding of various cultures, children will be far more likely to develop an appreciation for the values, customs, and traditions of the many peoples living within and outside of our borders.

Literature is a key resource in this effort. It is important to expose children to the literary heritage of cultures around the world: Native American, European, African, Asian, or Hispanic (Norton, 1990). All kinds of people should be represented in children's books that show many occupations, economic situations, lifestyles, and roles. Children need to be helped in developing a world view (Bishop, 1992). Traditional folklore from various sources can help children develop awareness of differing languages and cultural backgrounds (Piper, 1986). The range of multicultural books can also help children better understand themselves and their relationships to others (Tway, 1989).

But studying various cultures through literature can be difficult. An analysis of two recent lists of notable books shows why. In reviewing the *Best Books of the Year 1989*, a list of 55 titles created by Jones, Toth, & Gerhardt, only one book about Black Americans and one about Native Americans were included; there were none about Hispanics. Of the 67 titles on the list of Notable Children's Books for 1990 (Notable Children's Books Committee of the Association of Library Services to Children, 1990), only seven books relate to the African American, two to the Native American, and none to Hispanic cultures. However, there are people and organizations meeting the challenge. For example, the Association for Library Services to Children of the American Library Association (ALA) held a preconference meeting in June 1991 entitled, "The Many Faces in Children's Books: Images in Words and Pictures for Our Multicultural Society." The purpose of this meeting was to help participants learn about and celebrate the diversity in American children's books. (Information about this preconference is available from the ALA's Committee for the Selection of Children's Books and Materials for Various Cultures [(800) 545-2433].)

In addition, *Booklist*, published by ALA; the *School Library Journal*, published by R.R. Bowker Magazine Group; the *Bulletin*, published by the Council on Interracial Books for Children; *The Reading Teacher*, published by the International Reading Associaton; *Language Arts*, published by the National Council of Teachers of English; and *The Advocate*, published by Christopher-Gordon Publishers, Inc., all give special attention to books dealing with cultural issues. Also, Harris (1992) lists small and independent presses, large presses, organizations, journals, and a small group of bookstores that serve as good sources for multicultural children's literature.

In order to help teachers, librarians, and parents locate multicultural books more readily, we have included a multicultural literature bibliography in the Appendix. The books and other resources in the lists which comprise this bibliography are by and/or about people of color. These lists have been compiled using the same criteria parents and educators should use in selecting books for their children. The books presented to children should:

- neither generalize nor present specific images, either in text or illustrations, which establish or perpetuate stereotypes.
- show respect for a variety of lifestyles.
- be age appropriate.
- reflect and validate the culture.
- communicate messages through well-written, creative stories that the children will enjoy.

Objectives

Our book is designed to enable children to learn to understand and appreciate literature by and about people from diverse backgrounds.

Through completion of the activities included in this book, children will meet the following objectives:

1. Gain a sensitivity for the beliefs, values, and customs of others through well-chosen literature.
2. Understand and value the cultural and literary diversity that is part of our society.
3. Recognize that though there are differences, there are also many similarities among cultures: all children play games; people of all cultures celebrate holidays; everyone has basic needs.
4. Develop sensitivities to the common needs and emotions of all people.
5. Take pride in their own heritage.
6. Begin to understand the reasons why people from other cultures immigrated to the United States.
7. Recognize and gain insight into the prejudices and difficulties people of various cultures often face.

Applications

Read It Again! Multicultural Books for the Primary Grades is an activity book for children in grades one through three that is brimming with imaginative teaching ideas based on twelve multicultural books. These books are grouped within four sections: People of Asian Roots and Their Traditions; People of African Roots and Their Traditions; Hispanic Peoples and Their Traditions; and Native Americans and Their Legacy. In addition to an exposure to a variety of cultures, the activities in this book will help children develop skills in word recognition, story comprehension, and process writing. There are activities that involve children in drawing, painting, improvisation, geography, storytelling, mathematics, and cooking. Critical thinking skills can be developed by using the suggested discussion questions which reflect Bloom's Taxonomy (1956).

Read It Again! Multicultural Books for the Primary Grades is well suited to the classroom setting, library, or resource room. It can also be used in Chapter 1 programs and with children whose proficiency in English is limited. These activities, designed for a range of ability levels, can be adapted to large groups, small groups, or independent work.

This book is also an excellent resource for parents. The suggested books and activities will help parents establish their children's appreciation for other cultures as they are encouraging them to develop the skills necessary to become effective and involved readers.

Features

Introductory Activities: Each of the four main sections in this book includes introductory activities that provide children with a variety of broader insights into the cultures being studied.

Bibliographic Information: Names of the author, illustrator, and publisher as well as the publication date, number of pages, and appropriate grade level are provided for each book.

Summary: A brief summary of each story is included for the convenience of teachers, librarians, and parents.

Introduction: A recommendation for introducing each story in a way that will capture children's interest and set the stage for reading is included.

Vocabulary: Key vocabulary words, along with motivating ways to present them, are presented for each story.

Discussion Questions: Discussion questions to use during and after the reading of the stories are provided. These questions have been designed to foster higher level thinking skills.

Bulletin Board: Ideas for creating bulletin boards based on the selected books are described. Many of these boards call for participation of the whole class and require minimal teacher direction.

Activity Sheets: Three reproducible activity sheets are provided for each selected book. Many are designed to develop language arts, reading, and critical thinking skills. Others can be used to correlate the language arts and literature curricula with other subjects areas and to enhance a better understanding of different cultures. For flexibility and ease of use, the worksheets are arranged according to difficulty. Activity Sheet 1 is designed for use at the first-grade level, Activity Sheet 2 is designed for use in second grade, and Activity Sheet 3 is for the third grade. However, all three may be used by one child: Activity Sheet 1 could be considered an independent activity, Activity Sheet 2 as an instructional activity, and Activity 3 as enrichment. Based on the ability and interests of the child, teachers and/or parents will determine which activities are most appropriate to meet individual needs.

Vocabulary Listing: The Appendix contains a listing of all the vocabulary words introduced for the selected books.

Answer Key: Answers to several of the activity sheets are provided for the convenience of teachers and parents.

Related Literature: The Appendix also contains a listing of multicultural children's books.

Teacher Resources: Resources containing information about additional children's books and curriculum materials for different cultures also are listed in the Appendix.

Guidelines for Using This Book

Before using the activities in this book, it is important that you present the selected books in an interesting and meaningful way. When sharing literature with young children, it is vital that children enjoy themselves as they develop skills that will be of benefit to them when they read on their own. The flexible format of *Read It Again! Multicultural Books for the Primary Grades* allows the teacher or parent to use it in a variety of ways. The selected books and many of the activities can be presented in any order, although the following sequence is suggested:

1. Introduce the selected book.
2. Read the book aloud.
3. Ask the discussion questions.
4. Introduce the vocabulary words. Follow by rereading the story, asking children to listen carefully for these words.
5. Put up the bulletin board.
6. Introduce the activity sheet(s).
7. Select additional activities/ideas.
8. Allow children to enjoy the book alone as well as in a group.

But before you begin the four multicultural units presented in this book, we recommend that you select from the activities presented in the next section, "Setting the Stage." They are based on *People*, written and illustrated by Peter Spier.

References

Barringer, F. (1991, March 11). Census shows profound changes in racial make-up of the nation. *New York Times*, pp. A1, B8.

Bishop, R. S. (1992). Multicultural literature for children. In V. J. Harris (ed.), *Teaching multicultural literature in grades K-8* (pp. 39-53). Norwood, MA: Christopher-Gordon Publishers, Inc.

Bloom, B. S., Englehart, M. B., Furst, S. J., Hill, W. H., & Krathwohl, D. R. (1956). *Taxonomy of educational objectives. The classification of educational goals. Handbook I: Cognitive domain.* New York: Longmans Green.

Harris, V. (ed.) *Multicultural literature in grades K-8.* Norwood, MA: Christopher-Gordon Publishers, Inc.

Jones, T., Toth, L., & Gerhardt, L. (1989). Best books of the year 1989. *School Library Journal*, 35+.

Norton, D. E. (Sept. 1990). Teaching multicultural literature in the reading curriculum. *The Reading Teacher*. Vol. 44. No.1.

Notable Children's Books Committee of the Association of Library Services to Children. (1990). Notable children's books 1990. *Booklist*, 86, 1474, 1478, 1479.

Piper, D. (1986) Language growth in the multiethnic classroom. *Language Arts*, 63, 23-36.

Shweder, R. A. (1991, March 17). Dangerous thoughts . . . . [Book review of Carl N. Degler's *In search of human nature*]. *New York Times Book Review*.

Tway, E. (1989). Dimensions of multicultural literature for children. In M. K. Rudman (Ed.), *Children's literature: Resource for the classroom* (pp. 109-138). Needham Heights, MA: Christopher-Gordon Publishers, Inc.

SETTING THE STAGE

PEOPLE

Author
Peter Spier

Illustrator
Peter Spier

Publisher
Doubleday & Co., 1980

Pages	Interest Level
40	All ages

Reading Level
To be read to primary-age
audiences

Other Books by Spier
*The Fox Went Out on a
Chilly Night; London Bridge
Is Falling Down; To Market!
To Market!; The Erie Canal;
Gobble, Growl, Grunt;
Noah's Ark; Tin Lizzie*

Summary
People investigates the similarities and differences among the four
billion people on this earth. It emphasizes that while people are different in terms of eye color, shape and size, hair style, or country of
origin, we are all essentially the same *People*. Readers are introduced
to the games, hobbies, feasts, holidays, religions, occupations, and
foods of the world's diverse population. The book leaves the reader
"with an inspiring and lovely message not simply about the right to be
different, but about the excitement of difference" (David Hyatt, Former
President, The National Conference of Christians and Jews).

Introduction
Do you know how many people live on our earth? (Answers with vary.)
Let's find out in this book (hold up *People*). The answer will probably
surprise you. As we read, you're sure to learn some interesting facts.

Activities
After discussion, tell children that they will be making their own book
about people. Provide each child with his/her own copy of "My Own
Book About People" (duplicate and staple pages 4 to 13 for each
child). Go through the booklet, page by page, and talk about the
activities in which the children will be engaged. Set a pace for
children's completion of this booklet that is appropriate for individual
abilities.

DISCUSSION QUESTIONS

1 What were you feeling and thinking as we read the book? (Answers may vary.)

2 How many of the ways people are described in this book can you remember? Let's list them. (Answers may vary.)

3 According to *People*, there are 201 languages spoken on this earth. What are some different ways in which people communicate with these languages? (Answers may vary but might include compact disks, telegrams, FAX messages, computers, records, cassettes, telephones, communication satellites, walkie-talkies, signal flags, sign language, television, radio, etc.)

4 What if everyone in our class spoke a different language? What do you think a day in school might be like? (Answers may vary.)

5 Do you think it is important to learn about people who are different from you? Explain. (Answers may vary.)

6 People of different cultures do not eat the same foods. Why? (Though answers may vary, be sure children understand that an important reason is geography—people eat the foods they can easily obtain.) Now we can eat foods in restaurants that are enjoyed by people around the world—Chinese, Thai, Greek, French, etc. What foods of other cultures have you eaten? (Answers may vary.) What did you like about the food? Explain. Do you think people always agree about the foods they think taste best? Explain. (Answers may vary.)

7 The book *People* stated, "But imagine how dreadfully dull this world of ours would be if everybody would look, think, eat, dress, and act the same!" Do you agree? Explain. (Answers may vary.)

8 In *People*, we also read that some people are remembered long after they have died. What would you like to be remembered for? (Answers may vary.)

9 How are all people the same regardless of who they are and where they live? (Answers may vary.)

MY OWN BOOK ABOUT PEOPLE

Name _____ Date _____

MY OWN BOOK
ABOUT PEOPLE

Directions
Look again at the book *People.* Notice how many different people are pictured. Now, use pictures from magazines to create your own picture that shows that people come in many colors, shapes, and sizes.

Name _____ Date _____

Directions
Complete the following information about yourself. Draw
a picture of yourself on the next page.

1. The color of my skin is _____

2. The color of my eyes is _____

3. The color of my hair is _____

4. My hair is (curly, long, short, etc.) _____

5. I am _____ (inches, centimeters) tall and I weigh _____ pounds.

6. The words that I have circled below tell about me:

caring	wise	friendly	busy	bored
beautiful	foolish	quiet	lazy	unfriendly
intelligent	honest	noisy	kind	creative
ambitious	happy	sad	hard working	

Other words that might describe me are: _____

7. My favorite game/sport is _____

8. My favorite holiday is _____

9. The thing I do best is _____

10. When I grow up I want to be _____

From *Read It Again! Multicultural Books for the Primary Grades,* published by GoodYearBooks. Copyright © 1993 Liz Rothlein and Terri Christman Wild.

This is a picture of me.

Name _____ Date _____

Directions
Find out what country/countries your ancestors came from. On the world map below, locate the country/countries and color them. Note: Refer to a world map where countries are identified by name.

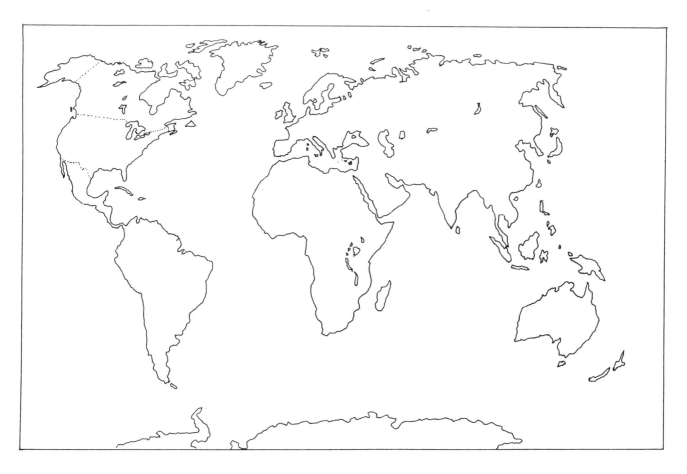

List the country/countries you have colored.

_____

_____

_____

_____

Name _____ Date _____

Directions
A cinquain poem has only 11 words.

Example

Line 1: One word (may be the title)   People
Line 2: Two words (describing the title)   All different
Line 3: Three words (an action)   Living all together
Line 4: Four words (a feeling)   Trying to get along
Line 5: One word (referring to the title)   Millions

Write your own cinquain about people below.

Line 1: Title   **People**

Line 2: 2 words about people   _____ _____

Line 3: 3 words about what they do   _____ _____ _____

Line 4: 4 words about how they may feel _____ _____ _____ _____

Line 5: 1 word about people   _____

Illustrate your cinquain here.

Name _____ Date _____

Directions
Bring in a recipe that is a favorite of your family's. Copy it on the recipe card below.

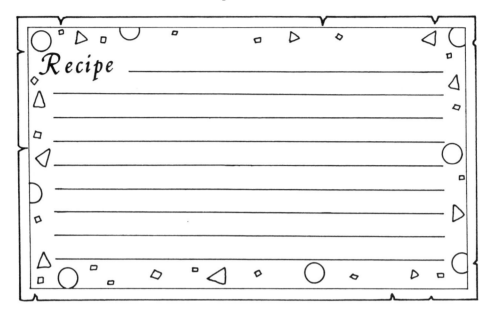

What is it about this recipe that you especially like?

_____

_____

_____

Draw a picture of what this food looks like just before you eat it.

From *Read It Again! Multicultural Books for the Primary Grades*, published by GoodYearBooks. Copyright © 1993 Liz Rothlein and Terri Christman Wild.

MY OWN BOOK
ABOUT PEOPLE

Name _____ Date _____

Directions
Ask someone who has come to America from another
country to answer the following questions:

Interview

1. Name of the person _____

2. What country did you come from? _____

3. What language is spoken there? _____

4. What do people like to eat there? _____

    _____

5. What sorts of clothes do people wear there? _____

    _____

6. What are the houses like that people live in? _____

    _____

7. Tell about a holiday that people celebrate there. _____

    _____

8. What sort of work did your parent(s) do there? _____

    _____

9. What do you like best about the country you come from? ____

    _____

10. Why did you leave your country? _____

    _____

Name _____ Date _____

Directions
Choose a holiday that has special meaning to you and
your family. Use the spaces below to tell how you
celebrate.

1. What is the name of the holiday you chose? _____

2. How do you celebrate this holiday? _____

3. Who joins with you in celebrating? _____

_____

4. What special food(s) do you eat on this day? _____

_____

5. Do you decorate your house for this holiday? How? _____

_____

6. What are some special games, songs, and/or dances that you and your family

enjoy on this holiday? _____

_____

7. What other special activities take place during this holiday? _____

_____

8. If you can, tell why and how this holiday was first celebrated. _____

_____

_____

From *Read It Again! Multicultural Books for the Primary Grades*, published by GoodYearBooks. Copyright © 1993 Liz Rothlein and Terri Christman Wild.

Name _____ Date _____

Directions
An acrostic uses the letters in one word as the first letters of other words. For example, an acrostic for the word "play" might be:

<u>P</u> icnic

<u>L</u> augh

<u>A</u> fternoon

<u>Y</u> o-yo

<u>An</u> acrostic for the word "math" might be:

<u>M</u> ultiply

<u>A</u> dd

<u>T</u> otal

<u>H</u> exagon

Write an acrostic that describes you, your family, or a country where someone from your family used to live. Use the letters in the word "people" as the first letters in your acrostic.

P _____

E _____

O _____

P _____

L _____

E _____

ADDITIONAL ACTIVITIES

Provide ample time for children to share their versions of "My Own Book About People." Then consider the following activities as a further introduction to multicultural education. It is not necessary, nor is it suggested, to use all activities included. Selection should be based on students' needs, interests, abilities, and objectives.

1 Obtain a list of pen pals from another country by writing to International Pen Pals, P.O. Box 2900065, Brooklyn, NY 11229-0001. Children can then write or dictate letters to those they select.

2 All children have at least one country from which their ancestors came to North America. Some families may have come to this country recently while others may have migrated years ago. Ask children to find out the names of the countries that members of their families once came from. Using a large wall map, designate these countries, matching them in some way with the children who named them. You may want to pin flags with the children's names on them on the appropriate countries, for example. Or, perhaps, you can string yarn from the names on a class list, placed next to the map, to the countries involved.

3 With the help of parents, organize an "International Day." Children can bring in favorite foods of various cultures. Dances, music, traditions, clothing, and other customs can be made a part of the celebration. (This would be a good time to share the children's "My Own Book About People.)

4 Arrange a day in which the children are requested to all wear the same clothes, such as white blouses and shirts with black skirts or pants. Make arrangements so that they will eat exactly the same foods for lunch and do exactly the same school work. Insist that they do things in the same way and, in general, follow all daily routines at the same time. At the end of the day, lead a discussion in which children talk about how they felt about this experience—about being so much like everyone else. Ask them if they would like everyone to be the same.

5 Create a display of items, objects, or pictures of everyday things that are made in other countries—coffee, cars, clothing, etc. Then discuss how different countries depend on other countries for many things which they use. Discuss how our lives would change if we could use only the things produced nearby.

From *Read It Again! Multicultural Books for the Primary Grades*, published by GoodYearBooks. Copyright © 1993 Liz Rothlein and Terri Christman Wild.

MY OWN BOOK ABOUT PEOPLE

6 Obtain a copy of *The Whole Earth Holiday Book* by Linda Polon and Aileen Cantwell (GoodYearBooks, 1983) or *Small World Celebrations* by J. Warren (Warren Publishing House, 1988). Share how various holidays are celebrated in different parts of the world. If possible, select one of the holidays and have a pretend celebration.

7 Using a calendar which has space to write beside each date, enter as many ethnic holidays as you and the class can name.

8 The National Geographic Society (Washington, DC 20036) produces a series of filmstrips titled "People and the Places Where They Live (No. 04333; 1981). This series consists of three filmstrips— "People in Mountains," "People in Deserts," and "People Near the Water." These filmstrips help children better understand people from around the world.

9 Invite members of the community who were born in other countries to visit your classroom and tell about the customs and traditions there. Encourage the children to ask questions.

10 Similar themes are found in folktales from different cultures. Obtain a copy of books such as *Yeh-Shen, A Cinderella Story from China*, retold by Ai-Ling Louie (Philomel Books, 1982) or *Lon Po Po: A Red Riding Hood Story from China* by Ed Young (G. P. Putnam's Sons, 1989). Read these stories and then compare and contrast them with the familiar Cinderella and Little Red Riding Hood stories. For additional folktale information, refer to the book *The Story Teller's Sourcebook: A Subject, Title, and Motif Index to Folklore Collections for Chidren* by Margaret Read McDonald (Gale Research Co., 1982), which provides an annotated bibliography of many folktales from other countries, such as "Cinderella and the Glass Slipper" from France and "Aschenputtel" from Germany.

11 Have children cut out the girl/boy pattern on page 16. Then using construction paper, yarn, buttons, and other materials, have them create a costume representing the country from which their ancestors came. Display these on a bulletin board entitled, "Our Melting Pot." Discuss with the children the diversity within the group.

12 Obtain "Skin Tones of the World" crayons from Chaselle Inc. (800-242-7355). This set of crayons consists of the following colors: mahogany, peach, tan, sepia, burnt sienna, and apricot. Children should use the crayons when coloring the skin of people. The crayons reflect the natural skin colors of people around the world.

MY OWN BOOK ABOUT PEOPLE

13 Order some multicultural dolls for display when studying a particular culture. The following sources have quality multicultural dolls dressed as contemporary children. Ask at your local school-supply store, or order a catalog by phone or written request:

Adoptive Families of America
3333 Highway 100 North
Minneapolis, MN 55422
(612) 535-4829

Heritage Key
6102 East Mescal
Scottsdale, AZ 85254
(602) 483-3313

Child Craft
P. O. Box 29149
Mission, KS 66201-9149
(800) 631-5657

Nasco
Box 901
Ft. Atkinson, WI 53538-0901
(800) 558-9595

Constructive Playthings
1227 East 199 Street
Grandview, MS 64030
(800) 255-6124

PlayFair Toys
P. O. Box 18210
Boulder, CO 80308
(800) 824-7255

First Step Ltd.
Rt. 26 RR 1, Box 1425
Oxford, ME 04270
(800) 639-1150

Pleasant Co.
P. O. Box 190
Middleton, WI 53562
(800) 845-0005

Hammacher Schlemmer
2515 East 43 Street
P. O. Box 182256
Chattanooga, TN 37422-7256
(800) 543-3366

Teach-A-Bodies
3509 Acorn Run
Ft. Worth, TX 76109
(817) 923-2380

14 Discuss the nationalities represented in your community. Write each of these groups across the bottom of a graph, like the one below.

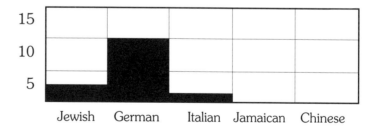

Next ask students to survey at least five people in their community/neighborhood to find out what nationality they represent. Then, compile the data collected, add or delete cultural groups on the graph, and draw lines on the graph to represent the number of people for each group.

15 Contact the Anti-Defamation League of B'nai B'rith, 823 United Nations Plaza, New York, NY, 10017, and request information on multicultural materials and issues. For example, the League has a publication entitled *The Wonderful World of Difference* which consists of 20 lessons (K-8) designed to help children explore the diversity and richness contained within a human family; multicultural audio-visual materials also are available.

16 Show the filmstrip *The Rabbit Brothers* by Robert Kraus (available from the Anti-Defamation League of B'nai B'rith, see address above). This is a cartoon filmstrip with an accompanying booklet about twin rabbits—Joe, who dislikes all rabbits different from himself and is miserable; and George, who tries to find some good in all rabbits and is much happier. Provide time for discussion.

17 Obtain a copy of *Chasing Games from Around the World* by Jan McPherson (Steck-Vaughn, 1992) and teach the children some simple games from other countries.

18 Obtain a copy of "Multicultural Cooking with Kids" [Lakeshore Learning Materials, (800) 421-5354], which contains 30 easy-to-make recipes. Help the children prepare some of the recipes and talk together about the culture from which the recipe originates.

From *Read It Again! Multicultural Books for the Primary Grades*, published by GoodYearBooks. Copyright © 1993 Liz Rothlein and Terri Christman Wild.

PEOPLE OF ASIAN ROOTS AND THEIR TRADITIONS

INTRODUCTORY ACTIVITIES

The following activities are intended as an introduction to our unit on people of Asian roots. It is not necessary—nor is it suggested—to use all the activities that are listed. Rather, they are intended as a guide to illustrate the scope of activities from which children can learn. Your selection should be based on your students' needs, interests, and abilities, and your own teaching objectives. Following these activities, you will find three additional sections, each focused on a particular children's book.

1 Using a large world map or globe, help children locate the following Asian countries: China, Japan, Cambodia, India, Indonesia, Korea, Laos, Pakistan, the Phillipines, Thailand, and Vietnam. Point out that China is the third largest country in the world geographically, while Japan, on the other hand, is slightly smaller than the state of California.

2 Invite people in your community who are of Asian descent to share information about their countries: legends, foods, crafts, games, dances, and so on.

3 Asian countries produce and export many items that are used in the United States. Ask children to look at labels and tags on clothes and various items around their homes to see where they were made. Most likely, they will find many product labels that will say *Made in China*, *Made in Thailand*, etc. Make an exhibit and/or list of all the things that the children can find that was produced by an Asian country.

4 Haiku, a form of Japanese poetry, is short and nonrhyming. Typically, a haiku suggests a mood or picture, often of a season of the year. A haiku is written with words totalling seventeen syllables, usually in three lines:

> Line 1: 5 syllables (the setting)
> Line 2: 7 syllables (the action)
> Line 3. 5 syllables (the conclusion or feeling)

> EXAMPLE: It is September
> Colorful leaves are flying
> Soaring high above.

As a group, create a haiku. Then, provide time for children to experiment with writing their own haikus. **Note:** If the children enjoy writing haiku poetry, you may want to introduce Tanka, another Japanese poetic form. A Tanka is a five-line poem with a syllabic pattern of 5, 7, 5, 7, 7.

PEOPLE OF ASIAN ROOTS AND THEIR TRADITIONS

5 Asian Americans have introduced the people of the United States to a variety of foods. Throughout the U. S. there are restaurants and markets where Asian foods can be purchased—Chinese, Thai, Japanese, etc. Obtain menus from several Asian restaurants and discuss together the many different foods they describe. Ask how many of them the children have tasted. If possible, have a tasting party in which the children have the opportunity to taste a variety of Asian foods. Compare the similarities and differences in ingredients, taste, appearance, etc.

6 Place a variety of books, pamphlets, pictures, and other information about The People and Traditions of Asia in a classroom reading center. A list of related books is provided in the Appendix.

7 Origami is a popular Japanese craft of folding paper (*ori* means fold and *gami* is paper). Help children make an animal face by using the following origami technique:

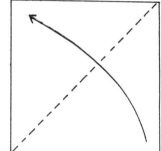

a. Fold a paper square in half to form a triangle.

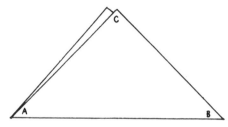

b. Fold the top corner (c) down so that the point extends past the baseline of the triangle.

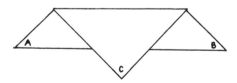

c. Turn up corners a and b to form ears.

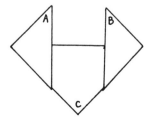

d. Draw a face to represent an animal.

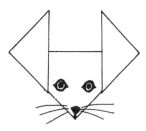 

Provide time for children to experiment with folding paper to create new shapes. **Note:** Make available other books about this art form, such as: *How To Do Origami* (1991), A US Borne book, Educational Development Corp., P.O. Box 470663, Tulsa, Oklahoma 74147, (800) 331-4418.

8 In many Asian countries, rice paper is used for writing letters, stories, or poems. Help the children make their own rice paper by following these directions:

a. Arrange flower petals, leaves or thin twigs on gray construction paper.
b. Cover with a sheet of white tissue paper.
c. Brush lightly over the tissue with a solution of glue and water, continuing until the tissue is thoroughly saturated.
d. Let the tissue dry. Allow the children to write a haiku (Activity 4) or a story on the "pretend" rice paper.

From *Read It Again! Multicultural Books for the Primary Grades*, published by GoodYearBooks. Copyright © 1993 Liz Rothlein and Terri Christman Wild.

9 Although the Japanese language, when spoken, is entirely different from Chinese, the Japanese have based their system on the one used in China. Teach the children a few words in both Japanese and Chinese.

Counting to 10 in Japanese:

Pronunciation Key: a=ah, e=eh, i=ee, o=oh, u=oo

English words	Japanese written form	Pronunciation
one	ichi	ee chee
two	ni	nee
three	san	sahn
four	shi	shee
five	go	goh
six	roku	roh koo
seven	shichi	shee chee
eight	hachi	hah chee
nine	ku	koo
ten	ju	joo

Singing Happy Birthday in Chinese

English words:	Hap py Birth day to you
Chinese written form:	Zu ni Shen ri Kuai ie
Pronunciation:	Zoo nee shen ree kwa lee

10 Help children work in groups to write letters to embassies in Washington, D.C., requesting information about China, Japan, Thailand, Vietnam, Indonesia, and other Asian countries. When all of the information is collected, allow the children to work together to create a poster, booklet, or bulletin board to display the information. Finally, allow time for each group to present "their" country.

Asia Society
725 Park Avenue
New York, NY 10021

Unicef
Children of Asia
331 East 38 Street
New York, NY 10016

Visual Communications
Asian American Studies Central
1601 Griffith Park Blvd.
Los Angeles, CA 90026

Once you receive the information, ask each group to create posters, booklets, or a bulletin board to display what they have learned. Allow time for children to share.

I HATE ENGLISH!

Author
Ellen Levine

Illustrator
Steve Björkman

Publisher
Scholastic Inc., 1989

Pages	Interest Level
30	Gr. 3

Reading Level
Gr. 1-4

Other Books by Levine
If You Lived at the Time of Martin Luther King; If You Lived at the Time of the Great San Francisco Earthquake; If You Traveled on the Underground Railroad; If You Traveled West in a Covered Wagon; Ready, Aim, Fire! The Real Adventures of Annie Oakley; Secret Missions; Four True Life Stories; If Your Name Was Changed at Ellis Island

Summary
Mei Mei immigrates with her family from Hong Kong to New York's Chinatown. She feels comfortable there because people look and talk the way they do in Hong Kong. But school is different—everything is in English. Mei Mei understands what she hears, but she refuses to use English. A new teacher finds a surprising way to help.

Introduction
Ask questions about children's experiences, such as: Have you ever moved? If so, where? What was the most difficult thing about moving? What did you miss about the place you used to live? Were there things about your new home that you liked right away?

Next, introduce *I Hate English!* by telling children that it is about a girl who moves from Hong Kong to New York. (Show them both locations on a world map.) Ask them to listen carefully to the story. How would Mei Mei answer the questions about moving that you just asked them?

Key Vocabulary
After children have enjoyed the story, write these words on the chalkboard and choral read. Then discuss the meaning of each word. Encourage children to use each one in the context of a phrase or sentence. Write their suggestions on the chalkboard.

tutors	lifeguard
argued	continued
twice	invisible
director	glared

Key Vocabulary Instruction
As you reread *I Hate English!,* have the students stand up and turn around once each time they hear one of the eight vocabulary words. Then turn to the sentences and phrases on the chalkboard that the children have dictated. Ask for volunteers to come to the chalkboard, draw a phrase around one of the key words, and read the new sentence or phrase about it.

DISCUSSION QUESTIONS

1 Mei Mei didn't know why her family moved to New York. Why do you think they might have moved? (Answers may vary.)

2 Why didn't Mei Mei speak in school? (She didn't like English and didn't want to speak it. She also was afraid she would lose something. Answers here might include her memories of Hong Kong, her ability to speak Chinese, etc.)

3 Why did Nancy say it was important for Mei Mei to learn English? (In America, almost everything happens in English.) Do you think it was important for Mei Mei to learn English? Why or why not? (Answers may vary.)

4 How did Nancy finally get Mei Mei to talk? (Answers may vary, but will likely include Nancy talked so much, Mei Mei wanted to talk, too.)

5 What are some special things Mei Mei told Nancy about Hong Kong? (She told her about Children's Day; Chinese New Year; her street and friends in Hong Kong.)

6 What would you have done for Mei Mei if she had come to our classroom? (Answers may vary.)

7 How would you feel if you were a new student in Mei Mei's school in Hong Kong? What new things would you need to learn? (Answers may vary.)

Bulletin Board
In *I Hate English!*, we learned about things Mei Mei likes and doesn't like. Divide a bulletin board in half. Label one side "We Like" and the other "We Don't Like." Ask children to use pictures from a magazine or pictures they have drawn to show what they like—foods, clothes, activities, places, etc. On the other side, they will show things they don't like. Ask them to print their names under each picture they select or draw. Talk together about the pictures. What are the reasons for the selections?

From *Read It Again! Multicultural Books for the Primary Grades*, published by GoodYearBooks. Copyright © 1993 Liz Rothlein and Terri Christman Wild.

Name _____ Date _____

Directions
Draw a picture of Mei Mei's face when she is happy. Write a sentence telling why she is happy. Then, draw a picture of yourself with a happy face. Write a sentence telling what makes you happy.

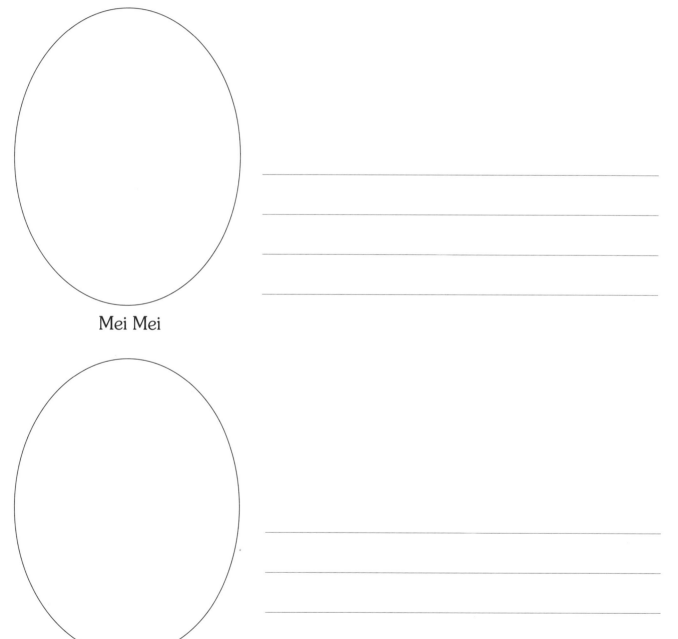

Mei Mei

Me

From *Read It Again! Multicultural Books for the Primary Grades*, published by GoodYearBooks. Copyright © 1993 Liz Rothlein and Terri Christman Wild.

Name _____ Date _____

ACTIVITY SHEET 2

Directions
In *I Hate English!* we learn about the things Mei Mei likes to do and things she doesn't like to do. Add to the list below using what you have learned in the story. Be sure to use complete sentences.

Things Mei Mei Likes To Do:

Mei Mei likes to play Ping-Pong and checkers at the Chinatown Learning Center.

_____

_____

_____

_____

Things Mei Mei Doesn't Like To Do:

Mei Mei doesn't like addressing her envelopes in English for the post office.

_____

_____

_____

_____

Name _____ Date _____

ACTIVITY SHEET 3

Directions
Where would you like to move? What would that place be like? Use this activity sheet to tell about it.

1. I would like to move to _____

2. I would like to move there because _____

_____

_____

3. It would be different from where I am living now because _____

_____

_____

4. The things I would miss the most would be _____

_____

_____

_____

On the back of this page, draw a picture of where you would like to move. Put yourself in the picture, too.

From *Read It Again! Multicultural Books for the Primary Grades*, published by GoodYearBooks. Copyright © 1993 Liz Rothlein and Terri Christman Wild.

ADDITIONAL ACTIVITIES

1 Invite someone into your classroom who has visited or perhaps lived in Hong Kong to speak to the students. Help children prepare questions ahead of time to ask the guest speaker.

2 Review with children how Nancy helps Mei Mei speak English. Go on to exchange stories about how teachers you and your students know have been helpful.

3 This story contains many compound words:

everything	shellfish	something
sometimes	lifeguard	without
understood	nobody	forever
homework	herself	anymore
everybody	goodnight	nearby
themselves	whenever	

Place these words on the chalkboard and help children see how they are formed from two words. After study, choral read them together. You can extend the review by creating a worksheet that calls for matching the parts of compound words.

Example:	shell	guard
	life	fish

4 In the story, Mei Mei writes a letter to her friend Yee Fong, who lives in Hong Kong, and asks if she, Mei Mei, could come back for a visit. Have students write their own letters from Mei Mei to Yee Fong. Ask them to think about what else Mei Mei might have written to Yee Fong when she first arrived. Did she tell her about the Chinatown Learning Center? Jones Beach? Her teacher, Nancy?

5 Ask children to write another letter to her friend Yee Fong now that she has decided to speak English. What will she say about the Chinese Learning Center, New York City, her teacher and her new friends now? As children share their completed letters, talk together about how these letters differ from the one Mei Mei writes in the story (and from those in Activity 4).

6 Show children the illustrations of Mei Mei throughout the book. Draw their attention to the changes they see in her from the beginning of the story to the end. Then ask them to draw their own.

THE STONE-CUTTER: A JAPANESE FOLKTALE

Author
Gerald McDermott

Illustrator
Gerald McDermott

Publisher
The Viking Press, 1975

Pages	Interest Level
30	Gr. K-3

Reading Level
Gr. 3

Other Books by McDermott
Arrow to the Sun; A Pueblo Indian Tale; Anansi the Spider, A Tale of the Ashanti; Daniel O'Rourke: An Irish Tale; Daughter of Earth: A Roman Myth; Tim O'Toole & the Little People; Flecha al Sol: Un Cuento de Los Indios Pueblo

Summary
Tasaku was a stonecutter. He was content with his work until the day he saw a prince go by in a splendid procession. Tasaku was envious and, when he returned to his hut, he wished that he could be wealthy, too. His wish was heard by the spirit who lived in the mountain. The spirit transformed Tasaku into a prince and he was happy for a time until he realized he was not all-powerful. The spirit continues to grant Tasaku's subsequent wishes in his quest for power. At its end, this Japanese fable points to the foolishness of Tasaku's ambitions.

Introduction
Have you ever read or heard a story in which wishes were magically granted? What was the story about? Who granted the wishes? Have you ever wished you could be something or someone different? If so, who would you like to be?

Today we are going to read a story that was first told in Japan long ago (point to Japan on a world map). It is about a man named Tasaku whose wishes to be something different are granted. The results are not at all what he expected.

Key Vocabulary
After reading the story aloud, write these words on the chalkboard and choral read. Then discuss the meaning of each word and use it in the context of a phrase or sentence.

stonecutter	lowly
mountain	wealth
demanded	transformed
obeyed	fragrant

Key Vocabulary Instruction
Ask students to bring in clothes hangers. Have each child cut out eight stone shapes from sheets of grey construction paper. Next, ask everyone to print one vocabulary word on both sides of each stone. Then give them thread to attach the "stones" to their individual hangers, creating vocabulary mobiles.

From *Read It Again! Multicultural Books for the Primary Grades*, published by GoodYearBooks. Copyright © 1993 Liz Rothlein and Terri Christman Wild.

DISCUSSION QUESTIONS

1 What tools did the stonecutter use? (hammer and chisel)

2 Was Tasaku's work as a stonecutter useful? (The stones he hewed were used to build temples and palaces.)

3 Why did the spirit grant him his wishes? (Answers may vary, but might include that Tasaku had never before asked for anything other than to work each day.)

4 Why do you think Tasaku wanted to be a prince? (Tasaku was envious. He wanted great wealth.)

5 Why did Tasaku want to be the sun? (He wanted to be powerful.) Was he happy being the sun? Why or why not? (Answers may vary.)

6 What did Tasaku do when he was a cloud? (He made violent storms. Fields were flooded and huts and palaces were washed away.)

7 When Tasaku became a mountain, a stonecutter chipped away at his feet. He trembled. Why? (Answers may vary.)

8 Which of Tasaku's wishes do you think made him most powerful? Explain why. (Answers may vary.)

9 Did Tasaku use his wishes wisely? (Answers may vary.)

Bulletin Board
Have students fold a sheet of 11" x 14" white construction paper twice. The folds will create four boxes. Have the students draw and label the things Tasaku wanted to be (prince, sun, cloud, mountain), one in each box. Place the completed drawings on a bulletin board entitled, "Tasaku's Wishes."

Name _____ Date _____

Directions
If you could be transformed into something or someone else, what would you want to be? Show how you would look by drawing a picture below. Then tell more about yourself by completing the sentence.

I would like to be a _____ because

then I could _____

_____

From *Read It Again! Multicultural Books for the Primary Grades*, published by GoodYearBooks. Copyright © 1993 Liz Rothlein and Terri Christman Wild.

THE STONECUTTER | Name _____ Date _____

ACTIVITY SHEET 2

Directions
Put a number next to each of these four pictures to show when it happened in the story. The first one is done for you. Below each picture, describe what Tasaku did when he got each of his wishes.

3

_____
_____
_____
_____

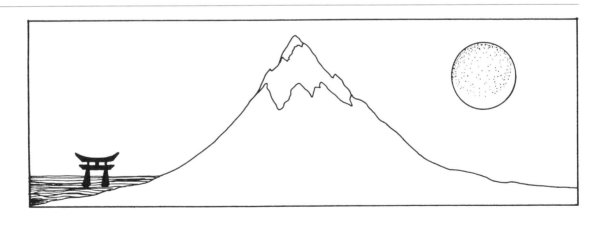

_____
_____
_____

_____
_____
_____
_____

_____
_____
_____
_____

THE STONECUTTER | Name _____ Date _____

From *Read It Again! Multicultural Books for the Primary Grades*, published by GoodYearBooks. Copyright © 1993 Liz Rothlein and Terri Christman Wild.

ACTIVITY SHEET 3

Directions
What would you do if you were transformed into each of the things Tasaku became? Tell about them in the sentences below.

1. If I were transformed into a prince/princess, I would _____

_____

_____

2. If I were transformed into the sun, I would _____

_____

_____

3. If I were transformed into a cloud, I would _____

_____

_____

4. If I were transformed into a mountain, I would _____

_____

_____

On the next page, draw a picture of yourself as either a prince/princess, the sun, a cloud, or a mountain.

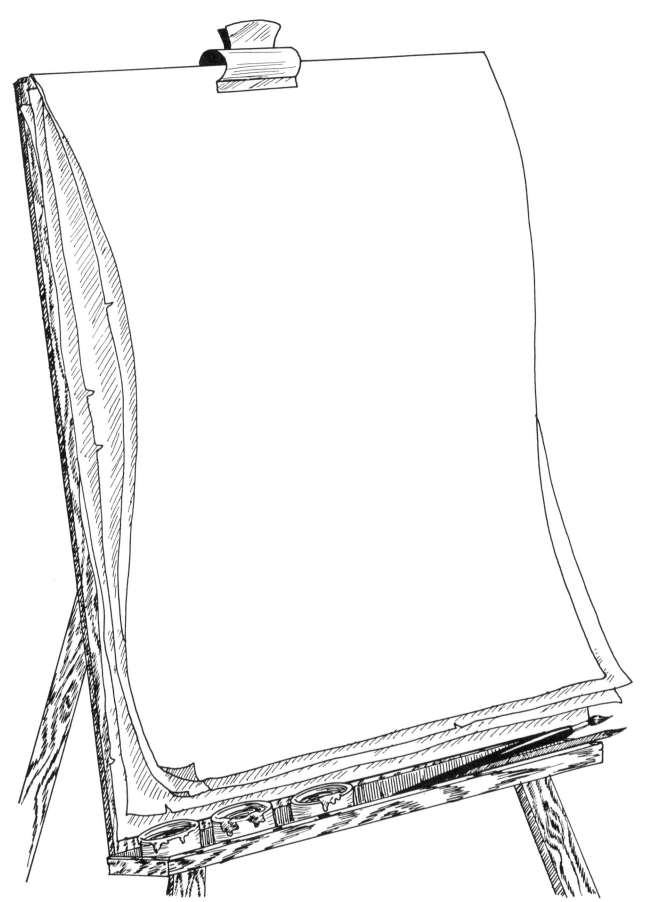

ADDITIONAL ACTIVITIES

1 Show children a different version of this story, *The Stonecutter: An Indian Tale*, retold and illustrated by Pam Newton (Putnam, 1990). Lead children in comparing it to Gerald McDermott's version. List together how they are alike and how they are different. Then survey the class to see which version children like best.

2 Tasaku believed that being a prince, the sun, a cloud, and a mountain would make him powerful. Have students create a list of the people and objects they think are very powerful. Encourage them to explain the reasons behind their choices.

3 The blocks of stone Tasaku chiseled away from mountains were used to form temples and palaces. Have the students draw and then paint something Tasaku's stones might have created.

4 Ask students to talk about statues they have seen—in front or on top of buildings, in museums, etc. Ask if they think it would be difficult to create these statues. Why or why not? Then discuss the fact that these statues are made in much the same way as the stonecutter made blocks for building temples and palaces. You may even want to show them a picture of Mt. Rushmore, telling them how and why it was created. If possible, invite a stone sculptor into the class to demonstrate the art of sculpting stone.

5 Demonstrate how you can carve a bar of soft soap into a new shape using a blunt plastic knife as a tool. Provide children with their own soap bars and plastic knives so that they, too, can try their hands at being sculptors.

6 Tell the students that *The Stonecutter* is a Japanese folktale. Read other Japanese folktales such as *Mouses Marriage* by Junko Morimoto (Puffin Books, 1988) or *The Two Foolish Cats* by Yoshiko Uchida (Macmillan, 1987).

7 What might have happened next? Ask the students to write another episode for *The Stonecutter* using the book to remind them what Tasaku was like. This can be an individual or a group activity.

THE WEAVING OF A DREAM

Author
Marilee Heyer

Publisher
Viking, 1986

Pages	Interest Level
32	Gr. K-6

Reading Level
Gr. 3+

Other Books by Heyer
The Forbidden Door

Summary
In a land far to the East there once lived a widow with three sons. She could weave brocades so skillfully that they seemed to come alive, and the widow sold them in order to buy food for her family. One day the widow saw a painting of a palace that she found to be so beautiful that she bought it rather than rice with her earnings. For the next three years she worked night and day to copy the painting into a brocade. But soon after it was finished, the brocade was swept away by the wind to the home of fairies. The woman's three sons set out, one at a time, to retrieve the brocade for their mother. Only one, the youngest, was willing to finish the perilous journey and return the brocade to his mother.

Introduction
Begin by asking children to tell about the most wonderful dreams they have ever had. Ask if they have ever wished that their dreams would come true. What changes would result? After ample time for sharing, introduce *The Weaving of a Dream* by telling children that this story was first told long ago in China (use a map to show where China is located). It is a tale of an old woman who worked very hard to make her dream come true. Show them the illustration on page 7 of the book. Ask children to imagine what the old woman sees as she looks at the painting. Write their predictions on the chalkboard. Then, give each of them a copy of page 39 of this book and ask them to draw a picture of what they think the old woman is dreaming about as she gazes at the painting. After children have heard the story, allow time for comparing their pictures with the illustration of the finished brocade. Discuss how their predictions were like (and unlike) the actual story.

Key Vocabulary
After children have heard the story, write these words on the chalkboard and choral read. Then discuss the meaning of each word and use it in the context of a phrase or sentence.

brocades	shuttle	fortune-teller	embroidered
loom	widow	weave	woven

Key Vocabulary Instruction
Keep the words on the chalkboard as you reread the story aloud. Tell children that each time they hear one of the vocabulary words in the story to quietly raise their hands, wave, and then put their hands down.

Name _____ Date _____

This is what I think the old widow sees in the painting.

DISCUSSION QUESTIONS

1 Why do you think the mother liked the painting of the palace so much? Would you have spent your money the way she did? (Answers may vary.)

2 Describe the mother's brocades. (Answers may vary, but they might include that the brocades had flowers, plants, birds, and animals on them.) What were they used for? (They were used to make dresses, jackets, curtains, and coverlets.)

3 Leje gave his mother the idea to do a weaving of the painting. Was this a good idea? Why or why not? (Answers may vary.)

4 How long did it take the widow to finish the weaving of the palace? (Almost three years.) During this time, the mother worked night and day on the weaving. Her eyes burned and she was tired. Have you ever worked on a project that you wanted to finish so much that you kept working until you were very tired? Explain. (Answers may vary.) Can you imagine yourself ever working as hard as the widow? Why or why not? If you did, what would you want to be working on?

5 Describe the directions given by the fortune-teller for getting the brocade back after the wind had blown it away. (She told each son to knock out two front teeth and put them in the mouth of a stone horse. After the horse had eaten ten berries, ride it through a mountain of fire and a sea of ice.) What would you have done? (Answers may vary.)

6 If you met the first two sons, what would you say to them about taking the gold from the fortune-teller instead of helping their mother? (Answers may vary.)

7 Why do you think the fortune-teller gave each of the first two brothers a box of gold? (Answers may vary.) What did they do with their boxes of gold? (Each went to live in the city.) What do you think Leje would have done if he had taken a box of gold? (Answers may vary.)

8 Leme and Letuie, the first two brothers, returned to their home to find a beautiful palace and garden instead of their hut. What did they do? (They crept away.) Why didn't they talk to their mother and brother who were sitting in the garden? (Answers may vary.)

From *Read It Again! Multicultural Books for the Primary Grades*, published by GoodYearBooks. Copyright © 1993 Liz Rothlein and Terri Christman Wild.

Bulletin Board

The widow in *The Weaving of a Dream* thought the best life for her would be living in a beautiful palace like the one she saw in the painting. Using the worksheet on page 42, have students create their own picture of what they would like their dream palace to look like. Place the caption "Our Weaving of a Dream" on the bulletin board and then display the children's illustrations.

's Dream Palace _____

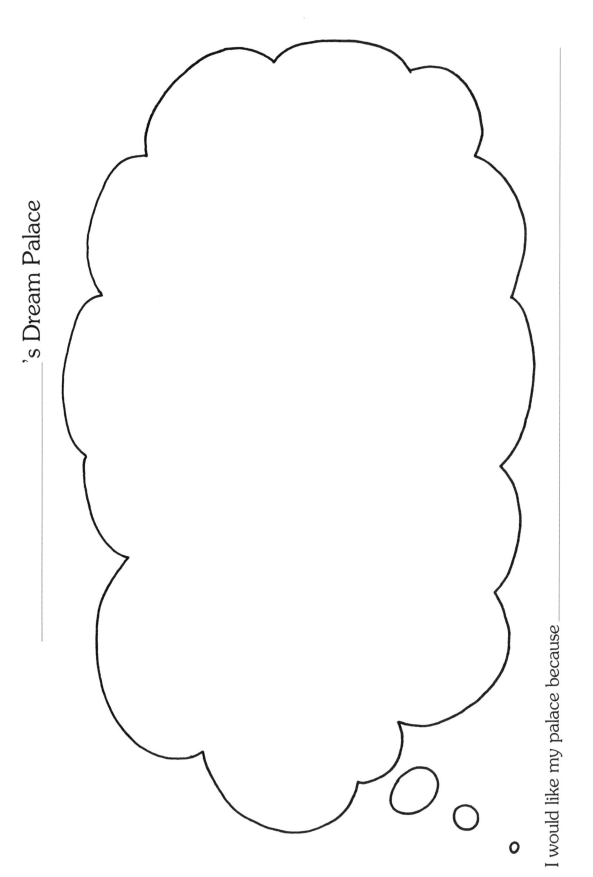

I would like my palace because _____

From *Read It Again! Multicultural Books for the Primary Grades*, published by GoodYearBooks. Copyright © 1993 Liz Rothlein and Terri Christman Wild.

THE WEAVING OF A DREAM

Name _____   Date _____

ACTIVITY SHEET 1

Directions

How would you describe each of the sons in *The Weaving of a Dream*? Place an X in each box that describes each son.

	kind	mean	clever	honest	greedy	caring	selfish	loyal	hard-working	good
Leme										
Letuie										
Leje										

How would you describe the widow? _____

_____

_____

THE WEAVING OF A DREAM

Name _____ Date _____

Directions

Some things in *The Weaving of a Dream* could happen in real life. Some things in the story could not happen in real life. Read the sentences below. Decide which events could really happen and which ones could not. Put an X in the right box. The first one is done for you.

	Could happen	Couldn't happen
1. The widow could earn money by weaving beautiful brocades.		
2. She could weave day and night for three years without stopping.		
3. The sons could earn money by chopping wood and selling it.		
4. A wind could blow the brocade away to the fairies on Sun Mountain.		
5. The sons would agree to help their mother.		
6. A stone horse would change into one the sons could ride.		
7. The widow's brocade could come to life.		
8. The two oldest sons could be sorry for the selfish things they had done.		

Write a sentence about something else in the story that could have really happened.

_____

_____

Write a sentence about something else that could not have really happened.

_____

THE WEAVING OF
A DREAM

ACTIVITY SHEET 3

Directions
Many things change from the beginning of this story to the end. Draw pictures in the boxes below to tell about some of these changes.

This is what the widow's house looked like at the beginning of the story.	This is where she lived at the end of the story.
This is how Leme, the oldest son, looked at the beginning of the story.	This is how Leme looked at the end of the story.
This is Leje, the youngest son, at the beginning of the story.	This is how Leje looked at the end of the story.

ADDITIONAL ACTIVITIES

1 *The Weaving of a Dream* is a folktale based on an ancient Chinese legend. Read other Chinese legends. Find other Chinese folktales to share with children. Jeanne Lee's *Legend of the Milky Way*, which provides an ancient Chinese explanation for the phenomenon of the galaxy, and Blair Lent's *Tikki Tikki Tembo*, in which the length of a name becomes problematic, are two excellent examples.

2 Lead children in making comparisons. Read Ed Young's *Lon Po Po: A Red Riding Hood Story from China* and/or Louie Ai-Ling's *Yeh-Shen: A Cinderella Story from China* along with the more familiar version(s). How are the versions alike? How are they different? Which do the children like best? Why?

3 As a group, write a new ending to this story in which the brocade is never found. Would Leje bring back the gold? Would the widow die from sorrow?

4 Reread the directions given by the fortune-teller to get to Sun Mountain where the fairies had the brocade. As a group or individually, create a modern-day version of getting to "Sun Mountain."

5 Display pictures of brocades or bring in a real one, if possible. Ask students to draw a pattern for a brocade they would like to have.

6 Ask students if they or anyone they know does any type of crafts such as weaving, knitting, quilting, carving, crocheting, or embroidery. If possible, ask some of these people to come into class to explain and/or demonstrate their craft. Also, set up an exhibit of any crafts that are available.

7 Discuss students' feelings toward the two sons, Leme and Letuie, who took the box of gold and went to the big city instead of returning home. Make a list of adjectives on the chalkboard describing these two boys (greedy, selfish, etc.). Next, ask students to describe their feelings about Leje, the son who returned the brocade to his mother, and make another list of words that describe Leje (caring, loyal). Finally, discuss the descriptive words they have used to describe Leje and have children arrange these qualities in the order they feel is most important for a friend to possess.

From *Read It Again! Multicultural Books for the Primary Grades*, published by GoodYearBooks. Copyright © 1993 Liz Rothlein and Terri Christman Wild.

PEOPLE WITH AFRICAN ROOTS AND THEIR TRADITIONS

INTRODUCTORY ACTIVITIES

The following activities are designed to develop children's appreciation for the many contributions we have received from Africa, its lands and peoples, as well as from African-Americans. It is not neccessary, nor is it suggested, to use *all* activities included. They are intended as a guide to illustrate the scope of activities that can be developed. Selection should be based on students' needs, interests, abilities, and your own teaching objectives. Following these activities are others related to three children's books—all tales from or about Africa.

1 The lives of many African-Americans throughout history are testament to their strength, courage, and resourcefulness. Read and/or make available books about African-American heroes/heroines such as *Martin Luther King, Jr.: A Picture Story* by Margaret Boone-Jones (Childrens Press, 1968); *The Day Martin Luther King Was Shot: A Photo-History of the Civil Rights Movement* by Jim Haskins (Scholastic, Inc., 1992); *Rosa Parks* by Eloise Greenfield (Crowell, 1973); *Harriet Tubman: They Call Me Moses* by Linda D. Meyer (Parenting Press, 1988); *A Weed Is A Flower: The Life of George Washington Carver* by Aliki (Prentice-Hall, 1965); *Jesse Owens, Olympic Hero* (Troll Associates, 1986) and *Jackie Robinson* (Troll Associates, 1985), both by Francene Sabin. Introduce each of these figures individually. Then, as a group, make a list of the characteristics each possessed that made him/her a hero/heroine.

2 Teach children to play the following game first played in Africa. Kasha Mu Bukondi (Antelope in the Net) can be played with a large group of children (the larger the group the better) inside or outdoors. To play, ask children to hold hands as they form a circle. Select one player to be the "antelope." The "antelope" stands in the center of the circle. As the group circles around the antelope, the children shout "Kasha Mu Bukondi! Kashi Mu Bukondi! (pronounced Kah-sha Moo Boo-koh-ndee'). Then the antelope tries to break out of the circle. When he/she breaks free, the others chase him/her. The player who catches the antelope becomes the new antelope and the game begins again.

3 Discuss how, for many years prior to the twentieth century, a number of African-Americans were not free (although there was a significant number of "free blacks" living in the United States during those years). They were slaves and had to do what they were told. Have children think about freedom and what it means—to others and themselves. In a column labeled "Freedom," ask them to list all of the freedoms they enjoy: freedom to eat, go to school, make friends, etc.

PEOPLE WITH AFRICAN ROOTS AND THEIR TRADITIONS

Next, ask them to think about which of the freedoms they have listed that they think are the most important to them. Number the items on the list as children prioritize them.

4 Obtain a copy of one or both of the following books and share with children: *All Night, All Day, A Child's First Book of African-American Spirituals* by Bryan Ashley (Atheneum, 1991), a book of 20 best-loved spirituals, and *Shake It to the One That You Love Best: Play Songs and Lullabies* from *Black Musical Traditions* collected and adapted by Cheryl Warren Mattox (Warren-Mattox, 1990). This set includes a cassette tape and songbook that is beautifully illustrated by Varnette P. Honeywood and Brenda Joysmith. Songs include: "Brown Girl in the Ring," "Kumbaya," and "Hambone."

5 Obtain a copy of Elizabeth Murphy Oliver's *Black Mother Goose* (Brooklyn: Positive Images, 1981) which contains traditional nursery rhymes illustrated by African-Americans. Use this book as you teach the children some nursery rhymes and show them the illustrations. You may want to compare and contrast the nursery rhymes in this book with those in other nursery rhyme books.

6 *Kwanzaa* by Deborah M. Newton Chocolate (Childrens Press, 1990) is a beautifully illustrated story about a family's celebration of Kwanzaa. Read the book and then plan a class Kwanzaa.

7 Obtain a copy of Ella Jenkins's cassette and guide of "Jambo" (available from Kimbo Educational, Dept. P., P.O. Box 477, Long Branch, NJ, 07740-0477, [800-631-2187]). Included on this cassette are response songs such as, "Counting in Swahili," and "A Train's a-Coming." Teach the children some of these songs.

8 Provide copies of the following books: Muriel Feeling's *Moja Means One: A Swahili Counting Book* (Dial, 1976) and *Jambo Means Hello: A Swahili Alphabet Book* (Dial, 1974). Help the children learn some Swahili words.

9 Obtain a copy of the record or cassette *Ethnic Dances of Black People Around the World* available from Kimbo Education (see above for the full address) which includes "talk through, walk through" instructions to eight dances, such as "Shango" (African Voodoo Ritual). Or, help the children learn some African dances by consulting the book, *The Dance of Africa: An Introduction* by Haris Petie (Prentice-Hall, 1972). *The Dance, Art, and Ritual of Africa* by Michel Huet (Pantheon, 1978) would also be helpful if you want to teach the children how to make costumes to accompany their dances.

10 Help the children learn about some of the African-American inventors and the products they invented. For example: Frederick Jones invented air conditioning units for trucks and boxcars, Richard B. Spikes invented the automatic gear shift, and Garrett Morgan invented the traffic signal. Discuss the importance of these inventions and encourage children to find out about other African-American inventors from books, friends, or families.

11 Request a list of African pen pals from the Afro-Asian Center, P.O. Box 337, Sugarties, NY 12477, (914) 246-7828, and ask children to select a pen pal. Provide time and encouragement for the exchange of letters.

12 Share books of poetry such as *My Black Me: A Beginning Book of Black Poetry* by Arnold Adoff (Dutton, 1974); *Honey I Love and Other Love Poems* (Crowell, 1978) or *Under the Sunday Tree* (Harper, 1988) by Eloise Greenfield; *Bronzeville Boys and Girls* by Gwendolyn Brooks (Harper, 1956); *Black Feeling, Black Talk, Black Judgment* by Nikki Giovanni (Morrow, 1970); or *Selected Poems of Langston Hughes* (Knopf, 1954). Allow time for the children to discuss the poems. You may want to select some of the poems to write on the chalkboard and ask the students to illustrate them.

TAR BEACH

Author
Faith Ringgold

Illustrator
Faith Ringgold

Publisher
Crown, 1991

Pages	Interest Level
25	Gr. K-3

Reading Level
Gr. 2

Other Books by Ringgold
Tar Beach is Ringgold's first picture book.

Summary

Cassie Louise Lightfoot is an eight-year-old girl who lives in an apartment in Harlem. One night, while on "tar beach"—the rooftop of her apartment building—the stars come down and lift her up into the sky. Once she begins to fly, she is free to go wherever she wants for the rest of her life. Flying makes her feel as if she has no limits. As she flies over the city, she sees many things, and she claims them as her own, including the George Washington Bridge, which her father helped build.

Introduction

Show the children the cover of the book. Allow time for them to discuss all the things they see. Then ask them to predict what they think the story will be about.

Key Vocabulary

After children have heard the story, write these words on the chalkboard and choral read them. Then discuss the meaning of each word and use it in the context of a phrase or sentence.

magical	hoisting	marvel	threatened
possession	claimed	member	tracking

Key Vocabulary Instruction

Give children a sheet of 11" x 14" drawing paper. Ask them to draw eight stars at the top. Have them place one vocabulary word in each star (copying from the chalkboard). Then, in small groups, in pairs, or individually, have them create a sentence for each vocabulary word on the bottom of the drawing paper. They may want to fill in a night drawing of the city between the stars and the sentences.

DISCUSSION QUESTIONS

1   How did Cassie feel when she was on "tar beach"? (She called it a "magical" feeling.) How did she feel when she was flying? (She felt free to go wherever she wanted to go.) Would you like to be able to fly? Why or why not? (Answers may vary.)

2   Where would you like to fly? Why? (Answers may vary.)

3   If you were on the rooftop of your apartment, condominium, or house, what would you see? (Answers may vary.)

4   What is Cassie's most prized possession? (George Washington Bridge) Why do you think it is her most prized possession? (Answers may vary, but might include: It opened the day she was born; her dad worked on the bridge; it has sparkling beauty.)

5   Why do they call Cassie's dad "the Cat"? (He can walk on steel girders high up in the sky and not fall.)

6   Why did Cassie have to take her baby brother Be Be with her? (He threatened to tell her parents if he couldn't go, too.)

7   Why does Cassie fly over the ice cream factory? (so she would own the factory—then her family would be sure to have ice cream every night for dessert)

8   Why do you think the rooftop of their apartment building is called "tar beach"? (Answers may vary.)

Bulletin Board

Have children create a quilt. Give each student a 5" x 5" square of cardboard. Ask them to use markers, colored pencils, crayons, pen, or pencil and create a design on their square that represents an event from the story. Place each square on the bulletin board touching one another, creating your class quilt.

From *Read It Again! Multicultural Books for the Primary Grades*, published by GoodYearBooks. Copyright © 1993 Liz Rothlein and Terri Christman Wild.

TAR BEACH

Name _____ Date _____

ACTIVITY SHEET 1

Directions

In the box below, draw what you would see if you flew over your neighborhood.

Name _____ Date _____

Directions

In the story *Tar Beach*, Cassie said that all you had to do was fly over something and it would be yours forever. In the box below, draw what you would like to fly over and claim as yours. Then, below the box, write what you have claimed and explain why you chose it.

From *Read It Again! Multicultural Books for the Primary Grades*, published by GoodYearBooks. Copyright © 1993 Liz Rothlein and Terri Christman Wild.

TAR BEACH   Name _____   Date _____

Directions
Cassie said that her most prized possession was the George Washington Bridge. Think about your most prized possession. Draw it in the box and answer the questions below the box.

What is your most prized possession?_____

_____

When did you get it?_____

_____

How/Where did you get it?_____

_____

Where do you keep it?_____

_____

ADDITIONAL ACTIVITIES

1 Have students each create a list of other things Cassie and her family could have done up on "tar beach." Share the lists aloud with the class, writing the responses on the chalkboard. Later, graph their responses on the board.

2 Discuss with students how Cassie had to take her brother Be Be flying with her because he threatened to tell her parents. Have students discuss good and bad things about brothers and sisters. Then have everyone write one thing they like about having brother(s) and sister(s) and one thing they don't like about it. If students do not have siblings, have them think about what they think it would be like to have a brother or sister. Would they like it? What wouldn't they like about it?

3 Read or summarize the information about the author, Faith Ringgold, that is at the end of the book *Tar Beach*. Be sure to tell the children that this is the first book she has ever written. Then, as a group or individually, write to Ms. Ringgold, telling her what the children liked about the book. If you like, mail the letters to her publisher, Crown Publishers, Inc., 225 Park Avenue South, New York, NY 10003.

4 In this book, the author talks about how her father couldn't belong to the union because his father, her Grandpa, wasn't a member. Then she says she will fly over the Union Building and claim it; then it won't matter that her father isn't a member of the union, or that they they say he is colored or a half-breed Indian. Discuss with children that sometimes a person treats another person differently just because those two people are not alike. The second person might have a different skin color, a handicap or disability, or might live in a different neighborhood. Tell the children that this is called "being prejudiced against someone." As a group, list all of the reasons why prejudice is wrong. **Note:** Use caution with this type of discussion, taking into account the community in which you teach.

5 In both *Tar Beach* and *Abuela*, the main characters fly over New York City. Compare and contrast these two books.

From *Read It Again! Multicultural Books for the Primary Grades*, published by GoodYearBooks. Copyright © 1993 Liz Rothlein and Terri Christman Wild.

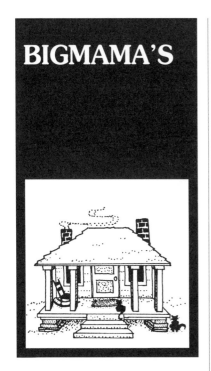

BIGMAMA'S

Author
Donald Crews

Publisher
Greenwillow Books, 1991

Pages	Interest Level
30	Gr. K-3

Reading Level
Gr. 2

Other Books by Crews
Freight Train, Trunk; Flying; Harbor; We Read: A to Z; Parade; School Bus

Summary
This is an autobiographical picture book that tells the story of Donald Crews's childhood visits to his grandparents each summer. Nothing changes from year to year, and the children enjoy their visit as they find their way around the farm.

Introduction
The author, Donald Crews, tells the story about the visits to his grandparents' house. He liked that during each visit, everything seemed to be the same as it was the year before. Is there a place that you like to visit? If so, why do you like to visit there?

Key Vocabulary
After children have heard the story, write these words on the chalkboard and choral read. Then discuss the meaning of each word and use it in the context of a phrase or sentence.

outhouse	stable	kerosene
lamp	bucket	station
porch	washstand	dipper

Key Vocabulary Instruction
Give each student a sheet of 8 1/2" x 11" paper. Ask them to fold the paper in half twice. After they unfold the paper, they should have eight boxes. Have children write one of the vocabulary words in each box. Then they can illustrate each of the words in the appropriate boxes.

DISCUSSION QUESTIONS

1 Why was the grandma in this story called Bigmama? (Answers may vary.) Do you think Bigmama is a good name for a grandmother? Why or why not? (Answers may vary.) Would your grandmother like to be called Bigmama? Why or why not? (Answers may vary.)

2 Do you think the conductor thought someone might leave a baby on the train when he said, "Don't leave no babies on this train"? (Answers may vary.) Why do you think he said that? (Answers may vary.)

3 Do you think this story happened in the last two or three years? (Answers may vary.) Why or why not? (Answers may vary.)

4 Do you think this is a true story? Explain. (Answers may vary.)

5 Where do you think the family that came on the train to visit Bigmama and Bigpapa were coming from? (Answers may vary.) What kind of a house do you think they live in? (Answers may vary.)

6 Would you like to visit Bigmama's? (Answers may vary.) Why or why not? (Answers may vary.)

7 Explain what is meant by the sentence, "In the backyard was the chicken coop, where "Sunday dinner's chicken spent its last day." (Answers may vary, but might include: They were going to kill the chicken and eat it for dinner on Sunday.)

8 Do you think Bigmama enjoyed having her grandchildren visit her? (Answers may vary.) Who else lived at Bigmama's? (Uncle Slank) What other family members visited? (The cousins came to dinner.) Do you like to have visitors at your house? Why or why not? (Answers may vary.)

Bulletin Board
Put the caption "Let's Go to Bigmama's" on the bulletin board. Provide 8½" x 11" sheets of paper and ask the children to illustrate what they'd like to do most of all if they were visiting Bigmama's. Place the pictures on the bulletin board and allow time for children to share.

From *Read It Again! Multicultural Books for the Primary Grades*, published by GoodYearBooks. Copyright © 1993 Liz Rothlein and Terri Christman Wild.

BIGMAMA'S

Name _____ Date _____

ACTIVITY SHEET 1

Directions
In the story *Bigmama's*, some of the furniture and some of the things the family did may be different than what you are familiar with. In the box below marked "Different," draw pictures of or write the words for things in the story that are different from what you know. In the other box marked "Same," draw or write words for things in the story that are the same as things you know.

DIFFERENT	SAME

From *Read It Again! Multicultural Books for the Primary Grades*, published by GoodYearBooks. Copyright © 1993 Liz Rothlein and Terri Christman Wild.

Name _____ Date _____

Directions
Read the sentence strips below. Next to each sentence, draw a picture to go with it. Next, cut out each strip on the dotted lines. Place the strips on your desk in the correct order. Once they are in the correct order, staple them together in the upper left-hand corner. You will then have a sentence strip book.

ACTIVITY SHEET 2

- -

The children dropped
a bucket into the well
to get water to drink.

- -

The family drove
with Uncle Slank
on a dirt road.

- -

The children
went fishing.

- -

The children
took off their
shoes and socks.

The family was
riding on
a train.

Bigmama and
Bigpapa were waiting
on the porch.

Name _____ Date _____

From *Read It Again! Multicultural Books for the Primary Grades*, published by GoodYearBooks. Copyright © 1993 Liz Rothlein and Terri Christman Wild.

ACTIVITY SHEET 3

Directions
Pretend that you are one of the characters in this story and have just returned from the visit to Bigmama's. Write a thank-you letter to Bigmama and Bigpapa thanking them for the visit.

(Date) _____

(Greeting) Dear Bigmama and Bigpapa,

_____

_____

_____

(Body) _____

_____

_____

_____

_____

_____

(Closing) _____

(Signature) _____

From *Read It Again! Multicultural Books for the Primary Grades*, published by GoodYearBooks. Copyright © 1993 Liz Rothlein and Terri Christman Wild.

ADDITIONAL ACTIVITIES

1   Tell the children to ask a parent, aunt, uncle, grandparent, or neighbor to tell them a story about somewhere they liked to visit when they were a child. Allow several days for the children to collect their stories. Finally, ask the children to share their stories with the class.

2   After the children complete Activity Sheet 1, discuss the things the children listed in the two columns. Point out that what is different in the story for one person may be the same for someone else; all people do not have the same kind of homes and live the same kind of lifestyles.

3   Discuss that this is a story about Donald Crews, the author, and his childhood visit to his grandparents' house. At the end of the story, he said that some nights he thinks he might wake up in the morning and be at Bigmama's for the summer. Ask the children what they think he'd see there. Then provide them with 18" x 24" sheets of paper and ask them to draw a picture of what they think Bigmama's house would look like today, now that Donald Crews is a grown man. Remind them to think about what might be the same and what might have changed. Allow time for children to share their pictures.

4   The family in this story had a lot of suitcases when they visited Bigmama. Ask children what they think is in the suitcases. Make a list on the chalkboard. Then, tell the children to pretend they are going away for a long summer visit and to think about what they'd want to take along. Allow time for the children to make a list of things they'd take. Then allow time to share and compare the children's lists with the list on the chalkboard.

5   It took three days and two nights on the train to reach Bigmama's. Then the family got off the train in Cottondale, Florida. Provide a map of Florida and help the children locate Cottondale. Ask the children if they have ever been to Florida. If so, what did they see? Finally, make a list of things the family might have seen as they looked out the window of the train.

MUFARO'S BEAUTIFUL DAUGHTERS

Author
John Steptoe

Illustrator
John Steptoe

Publisher
Lothrop, Lee, & Shepard, 1987

Pages	Interest Level
26	Gr. K-3

Reading Level
Gr. 2

Other Books by Steptoe
Birthday; *Stevie*; *The Story of Jumping Mouse*; *Daddy Is a Monster . . . Sometimes*

Summary
This fairy tale about two beautiful daughters was created by John Steptoe. It was inspired by a tale collected from people living near the Zimbabwe ruins. Nyasha is gentle and considerate while her sister Manyara is selfish and mean-spirited. The king invites the daughters of the Land to appear before him so he can select a wife. However, the king, in disguise, also meets Nyasha and Manyara. He is impressed by Nyasha's unfailing kindness and asks her to be his wife.

Introduction
Show children the pictures of Mufaro's daughters on pages 2 and 3 of the story. Ask them to study the pictures carefully and to describe first Manyara, then Nyasha, based on what they see. Write their descriptions on the chalkboard as they are offered. Then show them the illustration of the daughters with Mufaro. Can they add any additional descriptions? Tell them to listen carefully as you read the story. Were their predictions close to the actual characters?

Key Vocabulary
After children have heard the story, write these words on the chalkboard and choral read. Then discuss the meaning of the each word and use it in the context of a phrase or sentence.

daughter	village	worthy	honor
journey	servant	queen	garden

Key Vocabulary Instruction
Place each of the vocabulary words on a strip of tagboard. (You will want to make 2 or 3 strips for each word so that every child will have at least one.) Ask children to listen carefully to the sentences you are about to speak because they will include these vocabulary words. When children hear the word on their strip of paper, they should stand and read it aloud. Encourage them to use their words in their own sentences, too. Extend this activity by redistributing the cards. Perhaps you will want to include several of the words in the sentences you make up. For example, "The queen went on a journey to the village."

From *Read It Again! Multicultural Books for the Primary Grades*, published by GoodYearBooks. Copyright © 1993 Liz Rothlein and Terri Christman Wild.

DISCUSSION QUESTIONS

1 Why do you think Mufaro did not know that his two daughters were so different? (Answers may vary but might include the facts that Manyara behaved when she was around him and Nyasha was too kind to tell him.)

2 Describe the differences between Nyasha and Manyara. (Nyasha was beautiful, kind and considerate. Manyara was also beautiful but was selfish, spoiled, and bad-tempered.)

3 Which of the two daughters most wanted to marry the king? Explain. (Manyara, because she wanted to be the queen and rule over everyone.)

4 Why did the king select Nyasha over Manyara? (She always treated him well even when he was a snake in her garden, she also gave him a yam when he was a hungry boy and sunflower seeds when he was the old woman.)

5 What happened in this story that couldn't happen in real life? (Answers may vary but should include the king's disguise as a snake.)

6 How do you think Manyara felt when her sister became queen? (Answers may vary but might include feeling angry and disappointed.)

7 Would you like to have a friend like Nyasha? Explain. Would you want Manyara to be your friend? Explain. (Answers will vary.)

8 What kind of a servant do you think Manyara will be? (Answers will vary.)

Bulletin Board
Ask children to think of words (adjectives) that best describe Manyara. List these on the chalkboard. Now ask for adjectives that best describe Nyasha and write them on the chalkboard. Next, ask children to draw a flower blossom on a large piece of paper and print their first name in the middle. Then ask them to print the words they think best describe them on each of the petals. They should then cut out their flowers and help you cluster them on the bulletin board. Put the caption "(Teacher's Name) Beautiful Garden" on the bulletin board.

Name _____ Date _____

Directions

Manyara was so anxious to get to the king that she left the village alone to go to the city. Help Manyara find her way from the village to the city.

From *Read It Again! Multicultural Books for the Primary Grades*, published by GoodYearBooks. Copyright © 1993 Liz Rothlein and Terri Christman Wild.

Name _____ Date _____

From *Read It Again! Multicultural Books for the Primary Grades*, published by GoodYearBooks. Copyright © 1993 Liz Rothlein and Terri Christman Wild.

ACTIVITY SHEET 2

Directions

Mufaro's daughters were opposites. One was kind and giving while the other was selfish and spoiled. Can you match the opposites below? Read the words in the box below. Write the number of each word in the box next to its opposite under the box.

1. happy   5. round

2. cold   6. long

3. big   7. pretty

4. dark   8. girl

square _____   little _____

sad _____   light _____

boy _____   ugly _____

short _____   hot _____

Think of two more words that mean the opposite of each other. Draw a picture of each of the words in the space below.

_____   _____

Name _____ Date _____

ACTIVITY SHEET 3

Directions
Draw a picture of each of the characters in the ovals provided. On the lines across from each picture, write something that the character said. Be sure to use quotation marks.

Mufaro

_____
_____
_____
_____
_____

old woman

_____
_____
_____
_____
_____

Nyasha

_____
_____
_____
_____
_____

boy/Nyoka

_____
_____
_____
_____
_____

Manyara

_____
_____
_____
_____
_____

messenger

_____
_____
_____
_____
_____

From *Read It Again! Multicultural Books for the Primary Grades*, published by GoodYearBooks. Copyright © 1993 Liz Rothlein and Terri Christman Wild.

ADDITIONAL ACTIVITIES

1 The illustrations for this book were inspired by the ruins of an ancient city in Zimbabwe, Africa. Find Africa and then Zimbabwe on a map. Allow time for the children to discuss what the illustrations and story told them about this setting: its hills, birds, plant life, etc. How are all of these similar to and/or different from where you live? Then direct children's attention to what the illustrations tell us about how people once lived there.

2 *Mufaro's Beautiful Daughters* was inspired by a folktale collected by G. M. Theal in his book *Kaffir Folktales,* which was published in 1895. If possible, obtain a copy of this book. However, other African folktales are readily available, either in single volumes or in anthologies. Share several of these tales with children.

3 The names of the characters, Mufaro, Nyasha, Manyara, and Nyoka originated from the Shona language. The names have the following meanings:

> Mufaro—happy man
> Nyasha—merry
> Manyara—ashamed
> Nyoka—snake

Ask the children to find out if their names have any special meaning and/or how they got their names. Allow time to share.

4 Ask the children to think of other stories they have heard or read where a lovable, kind girl is rewarded for her goodness (such as *Cinderella, Sleeping Beauty,* etc.). Compare and contrast these stories with *Mufaro's Beautiful Daughters.*

5 Nyasha grew sunflowers in her garden and gave sunflower seeds to the old woman along the road on the way to the city. Obtain a bag of sunflower seeds to serve as a snack along with some juice.

6 *Mufaro's Beautiful Daughters* was a Caldecott Honor Book, an award received because of the quality of John Steptoe's illustrations. Ask children why they think the judges might have been so impressed by this book? then ask children to describe what *they* like about the illustrations. Bring in other books by Steptoe (such as *Stevie, Daddy Is a Monster Sometimes,* or *The Story of Jumping Mouse: A Native American Legend*) and lead children in comparing the way the illustrations are drawn. (There are a number of differences.)

HISPANIC PEOPLES AND THEIR TRADITIONS

INTRODUCTORY ACTIVITIES

The following general activities are provided as an introduction to the many cultural legacies of these diverse peoples. It is not necessary, nor is it suggested, to use *all* activities included. Rather, they are intended as a guide to illustrate the scope of activities that can be developed in multicultural study. Selection should be based on students' needs, interests, abilities, and your own teaching objectives. Following the activities are activities related to three children's books.

1 Obtain a copy of *Arroz con Leche—Popular Songs and Rhymes from Latin America* edited by Lulu Delacre (Scholastic, 1989), which is a colorfully illustrated bilingual collection of popular songs, games, and rhymes from Latin America's rich cultural heritage. Teach the children some of the songs and rhymes.

2 Some of the more popular foods that have been introduced in the United States as a result of the Mexican, Cuban, and Puerto Rican influence are tacos, enchiladas, tamales, tostadas, black beans, tortillas, fried plantains, etc. Bring in a menu from a Mexican, Cuban, and Puerto Rican restaurant. Talk with the children about the variety of foods on the menu and their familiarity with these foods. Then help children make tacos by following the recipe below:

Tacos
2 $1/2$ pounds ground beef or turkey
1 large onion finely chopped
1 head of lettuce shredded
4 tomatoes diced
1 pound grated cheddar cheese
25 taco shells

Brown the meat and onion. Put the meat mixture in a large eartenware bowl. Place the lettuce, tomatoes, and cheese each into individual bowls. Put the ingredients in a line as follows:

TACOS   MEAT MIXTURE   LETTUCE

TOMATOES   CHEESE   ONIONS

From *Read It Again! Multicultural Books for the Primary Grades*, published by GoodYearBooks. Copyright © 1993 Liz Rothlein and Terri Christman Wild.

Tell the children to make individual tacos by putting two small spoonsful of meat mixture in the taco, followed by two spoons of lettuce, one each of tomatoes, cheese, and onions. Enjoy!

3 Festivals and carnivals play an important role in the lives of many Hispanics. Popular dances include the cha-cha, conga, mambo, rumba, and the salsa. Enlist the help of the music and/or physical education teacher in teaching the children some of these dances. The art teacher could also be invited to help the children make instruments, such as conga drums and maracas to use as an accompaniment for the dances.

4 Set up a reading center that contains a variety of books, pamphlets, pictures, and other information about Hispanic Americans and the Hispanic culture. A list of related books is provided in the Appendix.

5 Invite people with cultural ties to Mexico, Cuba, Puerto Rico, and other Hispanic cultures to share with the children such things as the history, legends, foods, crafts, games, and dances of their countries. Allow ample time for questions and, later, discussion of the differences and similarities among the guests' presentations.

6 Some cities with large Hispanic American settlements hold annual festivals that feature arts, crafts, foods, and dancing. For example, a nine-day festival called Calle Ocho is celebrated in Miami,   Florida. Write to the Greater Miami Chamber of Commerce, 1601 Biscayne Blvd., Miami, Florida (305) 350-7700 and request information on the Calle Ocho festival. Then, as a class, conduct a Calle Ocho Class Festival. Invite parents and other classes to attend.

7 Help the children make a large class piñata. A piñata is a decorated container that is filled with candy, toys, or other surprises and then suspended from the ceiling rafter or tree branch. Celebrants are blindfolded and take turns trying to break the piñata with a stick. A piñata was traditionally used as part of the Christmas celebration in some Latin American countries; today it is also included by Hispanic Americans in holiday celebrations. To make a piñata, first have the children decide its shape (an animal shape, a ball, etc.). Then create this shape by covering a balloon(s) with papier-mâché until it takes on the shape selected. Be sure to leave a small hole in the piñata so candy and small toys can be placed inside. When the papier-mâché is dry, the balloon(s) can be broken. Fill the piñata, close the hole, and elaborately decorate it, using such materials as crepe paper and ribbon. Next, hang the piñata. Then take turns blindfolding one child at a time, allowing each child to have a turn at trying to break the piñata with the stick. Allow the children to help themselves to the candy, toys, or other surprises that fall to the floor.

ABUELA

Author
Arthur Dorros

Illustrator
Elisa Kleven

Publisher
Dutton Children's Books,
1991

Pages	Interest Level
34	Gr. 2

Reading Level
Gr. K-3

Other Books by Dorros
Tonight Is Carnaval; *Alligator Shoes*; *Animal Tracks*; *Feel the Wind*; *Ant Cities*; *Rainforest Secrets*; *Follow the Water from Brook to Ocean*; *Me and My Shadow*

Summary
Rosalba and her grandmother, her abuela, like to have adventures together. One day while they are at the park, Rosalba imagines that the birds they are feeding pick her up into the sky and she can fly. Her grandmother joins her and they fly over New York City. The sights they see are described in Spanish and English. A glossary of the Spanish words that are used appears on the last page of the book.

Introduction
Do you have a special relationship with any of your relatives—an aunt, uncle, grandmother, grandfather, niece, nephew, etc.? If so, what makes it special? What do you do together? What would you like to do together if you could? In this story, Rosalba has a very special relationship with her grandmother, her abuela. Let's read to find out what they like to do together.

Key Vocabulary
After children have enjoyed the story, write these words on the chalkboard and choral read. Then discuss the meaning of each word and use it in the context of a phrase or sentence.

flock	buildings
country	docked
harbor	downtown
factories	adventure

Key Vocabulary Instructions
Duplicate page 75 so that each student has a copy.

ABUELA

Name _____ Date _____

**VOCABULARY
WORKSHEET**

Directions
Write four sentences. Use a vocabulary word in each
sentence. Then draw a picture about each of the other
vocabulary words in the boxes.

flock	harbor	buildings	downtown
country	factories	docked	adventure

1. _____

2. _____

3. _____

4. _____

5.

6.

7.

8.

ntmlFrom *Read It Again! Multicultural Books for the Primary Grades*, published by GoodYearBooks. Copyright © 1993 Liz Rothlein and Terri Christman Wild.

READ IT AGAIN!
MULTICULTURAL 75

DISCUSSION QUESTIONS

1 Why does Rosalba's grandmother speak mostly Spanish? (This is what people spoke where she grew up.)

2 What made Rosalba think about flying? (She saw the birds in the park.)

3 Abuela loves adventures. What adventure does she want to begin at the end of the story? (She wants to go on a boat ride in the park.) What will they see? (Answers may vary.)

4 When Abuela saw the Statue of Liberty, what did it remind her of? (It reminded her of when she first came to this country.)

5 Why do you think Abuela likes being with Rosalba? Why do you think Rosalba liked being with Abuela? (Answers may vary.)

6 What things did the clouds look like to Rosalba? (They looked like a cat, bear, and a chair.) What things have the clouds looked like to you? (Answers may vary.)

7 Do you think Abuela likes living here? Why or why not? Explain. (Answers may vary.)

8 Did you learn any Spanish words? If so, which ones? (Answers may vary.)

Bulletin Board
Label the bulletin board, "Flying Over _____."
Cover the bulletin board with white paper. Have the students draw or cut out pictures from magazines to represent what they would see if they could fly over their own town, city, or community. Encourage them to look at the illustrations in *Abuela* to see how the illustrator has created a "bird's eye" view of New York City before they begin their pictures.

From *Read It Again! Multicultural Books for the Primary Grades*, published by GoodYearBooks. Copyright © 1993 Liz Rothlein and Terri Christman Wild.

ABUELA   Name —————————————— Date ——————

From *Read It Again! Multicultural Books for the Primary Grades*, published by GoodYearBooks. Copyright © 1993 Liz Rothlein and Terri Christman Wild.

ACTIVITY SHEET 1   **Directions**
Complete this worksheet.

This cloud looks like a ———————————————————

Draw your own cloud.
This cloud looks like a ———————————————————
Draw a cloud on the back. Ask a friend to tell what it looks
like to him or her.

ABUELA | Name _____ Date _____

Directions
Pretend that you can fly. Complete the paragraph.

If I could fly I would want to take _____
                                                    (person)

with me. We would fly _____
                                    (where)

We would see _____
                        (describe)

_____

_____

_____

_____

_____

_____

Illustrate what you would see.

From *Read It Again! Multicultural Books for the Primary Grades*, published by GoodYearBooks. Copyright © 1993 Liz Rothlein and Terri Christman Wild.

ABUELA

Name _____ Date _____

ACTIVITY SHEET 3

Directions
Complete this chart about Abuela and Rosalba.

Where did they go?	What did they see?	What did they do there?
the harbor	the Statue of Liberty	circle around her head

Which one do you think would be the most fun to see? Explain. _____

_____

_____

_____

_____

From *Read It Again! Multicultural Books for the Primary Grades*, published by GoodYearBooks. Copyright © 1993 Liz Rothlein and Terri Christman Wild.

READ IT AGAIN! 79
MULTICULTURAL

ADDITIONAL ACTIVITIES

1 Rosalba and her abuela live in New York City. Working as a class or in small groups, have your students think of the important sights, places, and buildings they could see if they flew over your town or city. This can be done through discussion, in writing, or in illustrations.

2 Have the students create a dictionary of Spanish words. They can staple 26 sheets of writing paper together and label them from A to Z. Ask them to list each word in both English and Spanish, and then write the meaning. They can get started on their dictionaries by using the glossary on the last page of *Abuela*. Encourage them to learn more about and then add words they hear spoken, too.

3 Have the students create a new adventure for Rosalba and Abuela. Their stories should include where they are going, what they will see, what they will do, etc. Have them illustrate their stories and read them aloud.

4 What country did Abuela come from? (We don't know.) We don't learn its name but we read that mangos, bananas, and papayas grow there. Using a world map, show children the places where Abuela might have grown up—places where these fruits are grown and where people also speak Spanish.

5 Ask a speaker of Spanish (a child in your class or elsewhere in the school or an adult from the community) to teach your students words in Spanish. Decide together what those words will be. Provide ample time for practice.

From *Read It Again! Multicultural Books for the Primary Grades*, published by GoodYearBooks. Copyright © 1993 Liz Rothlein and Terri Christman Wild.

FAMILY PICTURES • CUADROS DE FAMILIA

Author
Carmen Lomas Garza

Publisher
Children's Book Press, 1990

Pages	Interest Level
30	Gr. 1-5

Reading Level
Gr. 2

Other Books by Garza
No other books are known by this author.

Summary
The author of this book describes, through her illustrations, her experiences of growing up in a Hispanic community in Texas.

Introduction
Explain to children that this is a book of family pictures that were drawn by the author. Show the children the cover of the book and ask them what they think is happening in the picture. Ask questions such as: Who are the people in this picture? What are they doing? Would they like to be in this picture? What would they want to be doing if they were in the picture?

Key Vocabulary
After children have enjoyed the story, write these words on the chalkboard and choral read. Then discuss the meaning of each word and use it in the context of a phrase or sentence.

Mexico	nopal cactus	shark
cakewalk	mesquite	tortillas
tamales	curandera	

Key Vocabulary Instruction
Introduce and reinforce the vocabulary by writing the vocabulary words on 3" x 5" index cards and then play the cakewalk game that is described on pages 12 and 13 of the book. Place the vocabulary words face down alongside the numbers. When the music stops, ask the children to pick up the vocabulary word cards, holding them up for the group to see. Then ask the children to go around the circle as they choral read the words.

DISCUSSION QUESTIONS

1 Which of the family pictures did you most like reading about? Why? (Answers may vary.)

2 Have you ever done something that is similar to an event described in this book? Is so, what? (Answers may vary.)

3 Which of the events described in this story do you think would have been the most fun? Why? (Answers may vary.)

4 Which of the events described in the story do you think was the most unusual or different? (Answers may vary.)

5 Who is telling this story? (Carmen Lomas Garza, the author) Do you think she does a good job telling the story? Why or why not? (Answers may vary.)

6 Describe the family in the story. Would you like to be part of this family? (Answers may vary.) Explain.

7 How does this story make you feel? (Answers may vary.) Explain.

8 What do you think is the most important event in the story? (Answers may vary.) Explain.

Bulletin Board
Place the heading "We Are a Family" on the bulletin board. Tell the children to bring in a baby pictures of themselves. Adhere the pictures to the bulletin board and number the pictures. Ask the children to write the numbers on a sheet of paper and write down the names of the children they recognize by the appropriate numbers.

From *Read It Again! Multicultural Books for the Primary Grades*, published by GoodYearBooks. Copyright © 1993 Liz Rothlein and Terri Christman Wild.

FAMILY PICTURES •
CUADROS DE
FAMILIA

Name _____ Date _____

ACTIVITY SHEET 1

Directions

In the book *Family Pictures*, the author illustrated events that she remembered doing with her family when she was a young girl. In the box below, draw a picture of something you would like to do or have done with your family.

_____'s Family Picture

FAMILY PICTURES • CUADROS DE FAMILIA

ACTIVITY SHEET 2

Directions

In the box labeled "Different," draw one event that you do with your family that is different from an event the author did with her family. In the box beside the picture, write about the event. In the box labeled "Same," draw one event that you do with your family that is the same as an event the author did with her family. In the box beside that picture, tell how the events are alike.

Different

Same

From *Read It Again! Multicultural Books for the Primary Grades*, published by GoodYearBooks. Copyright © 1993 Liz Rothlein and Terri Christman Wild.

FAMILY PICTURES •
CUADROS DE
FAMILIA

Name _____ Date _____

ACTIVITY SHEET 3

Directions

The author of *Family Pictures* illustrated the events she remembered about the years when she was growing up. Think about events of your life so far and complete the following statements:

1. The one thing that has happened so far in my life that I remember most of all

was _____

_____

_____

2. I was _____ years old.

3. The people that were with me were _____

_____

_____

4. I liked/disliked "the happening" because _____

_____

_____

5. Something that I'd like to have happen in my life as I am growing up is _____

_____

_____

ADDITIONAL ACTIVITIES

1 Divide the children into groups of 4 or 5. Ask each group to select one of the "family pictures" from this story and to dramatize it. Allow time for them to practice and develop a dialogue. Then ask each group to act out their "family picture" as the others guess which picture it is.

2 On the back cover of the book there is a self-portrait of the author, Carmen Lomas Garza. Show this to the children. Then ask them to make self-portraits of themselves. Allow time to share.

3 The author of this story said that she knew when she was 13 years old that she wanted to be an artist. Have a discussion about what the children think they might like to be when they grow up. Make a list of careers on the chalkboard, making tally marks by those mentioned more than once. Finally, make a graph of possible careers for the children.

4 One of the "family pictures" was the author's sixth birthday party. She had a piñata to break. Using directions in Introductory Activity #7 for this unit, help the children make a piñata and let them take turns trying to break it.

5 Ask the children to bring in a picture of themselves and their families or friends doing something together. Point out that it can be of them working or playing together. Allow time for them to share the picture and describe the event.

6 In this story, they played a game called "cakewalk" to raise money. Let the children help you to make a circle similar to the one on page 13 of the book. Then play the game, following the directions on page 12 of the book. Use cupcakes or muffins for prizes.

7 The author of the book grew up in Kingsville, Texas. Help the children locate Kingsville on a Texas map. Discuss how life in Kingsville, Texas, is similar and how it is different from where they live. The illustrations in the book can help with this activity.

From *Read It Again! Multicultural Books for the Primary Grades*, published by GoodYearBooks. Copyright © 1993 Liz Rothlein and Terri Christman Wild.

NINE DAYS TO CHIRSTMAS

Author
Marie Hall Ets and Aurora Labastida

Illustrator
Marie Hall Ets

Publisher
Viking Children's Books (Reissue), 1991

Pages	Interest Level
44	Gr. 2

Reading Level
Gr. 2-3

Other Books by Marie Hall Ets
Gilberto and the Wind; In the Forest; Just Me; Play with Me

Summary
Ceci is old enough to have her first posada. A posada is a special Mexican party given on each of the nine nights before Chrismas. Ceci chooses a piñata in the shape of a star which will be used during the party celebrations, but when it comes time for her and the guests to break it, she is dismayed. Ceci wants to keep her beautiful piñata just as it is. But something magical happens. Though the piñata is broken, a new star appears and speaks to Ceci before it flies up to the sky. The star is Ceci's Christmas gift to the world.

Introduction
What party have you given or gone to lately? How did everyone get ready? What makes a party day different from other days? What do you like about parties? In *Nine Days to Christmas*, you will hear how everyone gets ready for a posada. A posada is a special party given on each of the nine nights before Christmas. As you listen, think about how Ceci's party is like ones you have been to. How is it different?

Key Vocabulary
After children have enjoyed the story, introduce and discuss the meanings of the following words.

listened	disappeared	scrambling	knocked
whispered	blinking	shouting	entered

Key Vocabulary Instruction
The vocabulary words are all verbs. Tell the students that a verb is a word that shows action. Write each of the eight vocabulary words on an index card. Place the eight cards in a bowl/basket. Ask a student to select one card and have him/her act out the action word without talking. Once someone in the classroom has guessed the vocabulary word, he/she may come up and pull out a word. The game continues until all eight words have been acted out and correctly identified.

DISCUSSION QUESTIONS

1 Why do you think Ceci was so excited about having a posada? (Answers may vary, but might include: It was her first one, she would have had a piñata, all the village people would come, etc.)

2 When Ceci's mother went to the market, Ceci sat down by the gate in front of their house and watched what was happening in the street. Describe what she saw. (Answers may vary.) What do you see when you stand out in front of your house/apartment? (Answers may vary.)

3 What are piñatas made of? (papier-mâché) Looking at the piñatas on pages 28 to 33, decide which one you would like. Why? (Answers may vary.)

4 Why did Ceci take a bath instead of a nap? (Though answers may vary, she was thinking about the ducks in the park and wanted to know how it felt to be a duck sitting on the water.)

5 Ceci's mother was afraid she might have caught a cold by getting into a bath filled with cold water. Have you ever frightened your mother by something you've done? If so, explain. (Answers may vary.)

6 Why did all the piñatas want Ceci to choose them? (Answers may vary, but might include that they heard wonderful things often happened to piñatas chosen by little girls for their first posadas.)

7 What happens in this story that couldn't happen in real life? (The piñatas and the star spoke to Ceci.) Do you like to read stories about magical things and happenings? (Answers may vary.)

8 What did you learn about Mexico in this story? (Answers may vary.)

Bulletin Board
Entitle the bulletin board "Possible Piñatas." Give the students a large sheet (11" x 14") of white construction paper, and have them design and color a piñata. (Show students pages 28–33 of *Nine Days to Christmas* if they need help coming up with an idea.) Under the pictures, ask students to list what they would place inside their piñatas.

From *Read It Again! Multicultural Books for the Primary Grades*, published by GoodYearBooks. Copyright © 1993 Liz Rothlein and Terri Christman Wild.

Name _____   Date _____

Directions
Read the sentence about Ceci in each box. Then draw a picture about it.

Ceci is picking out a piñata.	Ceci is taking a bath.
Ceci is filling her piñata.	Ceci is dressed up in her village costume.

Name _____   Date _____

Directions
Pretend you are having a party. Make an invitation for your party. Don't forget to decorate it.

Please come to my _____

Name: _____

Place: _____

Date: _____

Time: _____

Telephone: _____

Name _____ Date _____

ACTIVITY SHEET 3

Directions
Compare where you live and what you do with where
Ceci lives and what she does.

Things that are the same:

_____

_____

_____

_____

Things that are different:

_____

_____

_____

_____

What would you like most about living in Mexico?

_____

_____

_____

_____

_____

ADDITIONAL ACTIVITIES

1 Have a posada in your classroom. Create or buy a piñata and decide together how it should be filled. The students can sing songs and play games. Perhaps they will want to wear costumes.

2 At the end of this story, the children break Ceci's piñata. Ceci is sad until she hears a voice and looks up in the sky. Her star-shaped piñata has become a real star. Have the students select another piñata and create a new ending for the story. (This can be an individual or group activity.)

3 Discuss the similarities and differences in the way Ceci and her family celebrate Christmas and the way the students in your class celebrate theirs (or another special holiday). Then ask students to each draw a Venn diagram as illustrated below. Tell them to fill one circle with words or phrases that describe Ceci's Christmas. In the other circle, they can fill in words or phrases to describe their special day. In the space where the circles overlap, ask them to write words or phrases that are similar to both celebrations.

Venn Diagram

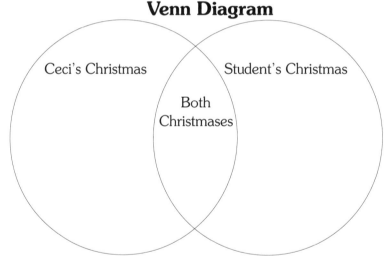

Ceci's Christmas

Student's Christmas

Both
Christmases

4 In *Nine Days to Christmas*, Ceci and Maria buy tortillas from two old women. Explain to the students that tortillas are a basic bread in Mexico. Using the following recipe, help the students make tortillas.

> 4 cups of masa harina (fine corn flour)
> 2 cups water

Mix the water and masa harina together. Then have the students make small balls and press them flat until they are thin and round. Heat a large ungreased skillet or griddle. Drop tortillas (one at a time) onto the skillet. Brown on one side and then the other. Serve with butter or beans.

NINE DAYS TO CHRISTMAS

5 Use *Subject Guide to Children's Books in Print* (a reference found in nearly every public library) to help you locate books about Mexico that match your students' interests and abilities. (The listings include recommended grade designations.) Present these materials to children. Help them discover how this diverse country is like and unlike our own.

6 Ask someone who celebrates Christmas with the traditional posada to visit your classroom and share experiences. Prepare children in advance by helping them think of questions they would like answered about this special celebration.

NATIVE AMERICANS AND THEIR LEGACY

INTRODUCTORY ACTIVITIES

The following activities are provided as an introduction to the unit on Native Americans. It is not necessary, nor is it suggested, to use *all* activities included. Rather, they are intended as a guide to illustrate the scope of activities that can be developed in multicultural study. Selection should be based on students' needs, interests, abilities, and your own teaching objectives. Following the general activities are activities related to three children's books.

1 Help children compose a class letter to be sent to the United States Bureau of Indian Affairs or to an area office of the Bureau requesting information on Native Americans: How many Native Americans are living in the United States today? Where do they live? What resources are available to learn more about them? The addresses are:

United States Department of the Interior
Bureau of Indian Affairs
1951 Constitution Avenue, N.W.
Washington, DC 20245

Area Offices:

Area	Address
Aberdeen, SD	115 Fourth Ave., SE., 57401
Albuquerque, NM	P.O. Box 26567,
	615 N. 1st St., 87125-6567
Anadarko, OK	P.O. Box 368, 73005
Billings, MT	316 N. 26th St., 59101
Juneau, AK	Box 3-8000. 99802
Minneapolis, MN	15 S. 5th St., 55402
Muskogee, OK	Old Federal Bldg., 77401
Phoenix, AZ	P.O. Box 7007, 3030 N. Central, 85011
Portland, OR	P.O. Box 3785, 1425 NE Irving St., 97208
Sacramento, CA	2800 Cottage Way, 95825

2 Invite Native Americans to your classroom to share with the children such things as their tribal history, legends, foods, crafts, games, and dances. Allow time for ample discussion and questions.

3 Obtain a set of the "Indian Tribes" tapes found in *Think: Listen and Learn Skill Kit* (Troll Associates, 1979). Set up a listening center with cassette recorders and earphones. Provide time for the children to listen to the tapes. Ask them to keep a listening log indicating the date they listened to each tape and comments about what they learned. Allow time to share.

NATIVE AMERICANS AND THEIR LEGACY

4 Show the video *Legend of the Indians: The Legend of the Corn* (Films for Humanities, Inc., 1985). Lead children in discussing what they have viewed. Then ask each to write a short story on how they would have liked to have lived with the Indians during this period of time. (Other films, videos, and filmstrips are available from the Navajo Tribe, Window Rock, AZ 86515.)

5 Allow children to experiment with dance movements that correspond with the music found in resources such as the book and record *Dance-A-Story About the Brave Hunter* by Paul and Anne Barlin (Ginn and Company, 1965); musical selections from "Songs of Earth, Water, Fire, and Sky" on *Music of the American Indians* (New World Records, 1965); "Maori Indian Chants" from Ella Jenkins's *You'll Sing a Song and I'll Sing a Song* (Smithsonian Folkways Records, 1989); *Authentic Indian Dances and Folklore* by Michigan Chippewa Chiefs (available from Kimbo Educational Records, P. O. Box 246, Deal, NJ 07723).

6 Take the class on a field trip to a local museum that provides a display of Native American artifacts. Ask children to draw pictures and take notes about things they see while in the museum. When you return to the classroom, ask them to illustrate the display they found to be most interesting and write a brief paragraph describing it. Compile the papers into a class booklet entitled "Our Trip to the Museum."

7 Discuss with the class that many Indians used various signs as a way to communicate. Use *Indian Sign Language* by Robert Hofsinde (Morrow, 1956) as a guide to help the children learn some sign language.

8 Obtain an ethnological map called "Indians in North America" (National Geographic Society, 1982) and then display it on the wall. As different tribes are introduced, locate the places where they have lived and/or currently live on the map.

9 Set up a reading center that contains a variety of books, pamphlets, pictures, and other information about Native Americans. A list of related books is provided in the Appendix.

ANNIE AND THE OLD ONE

Author
Miska Miles

Illustrator
Peter Parnell

Publisher
Little, Brown & Co., 1971

Pages	Interest Level
44	K -3

Reading Level
Gr. 2

Other Books by Miles
Gertrude's Pocket; Apricot ABC

Summary
Annie lives with her mother, father, and grandmother—the Old One—in a hogan. This Navajo family leads a traditional life in many ways: Annie's mother weaves rugs, her father makes jewelry, and the family tends sheep. Annie's relationship with her grandmother is a close one. When the Old One tells the family that she will go to Mother Earth, Annie is dismayed. Grandmother then teaches her about life's cycles. Annie grows in her new understanding.

Introduction
This is a story about the fun Annie, a little girl, and her grandmother had together. The grandmother always seems to have time for Annie. Annie couldn't imagine life without her. Tell us about an elderly person you know and feel close to. What do you do together? What do you talk about? What has that person taught you? Annie's grandmother helps her understand something that is very important. Let's read to learn what that is.

Key Vocabulary
After the children have heard the story, write these words on the chalkboard and choral read. Then discuss the meaning of each word and use it in the context of a phrase or sentence.

coyote	weave	mesa	warp
desert	Navajo	hogan	loom

Key Vocabulary Instruction
Tell the children that you are going to give them some clues about the key vocabulary words. They should use these clues to find the words you are thinking of on the chalkboard.

Clues: I'm thinking of

what the Indians call their homes (hogans)
a name of an Indian tribe (Navajo)
an animal that lives in the southwestern part of our country (coyotye)
the low land near Annie's hogan (mesa)
what the mother did her weaving on (loom)
the strings that went up and down on the loom (warp)
something the mother and grandmother did that they wanted to— teach Annie (weave)
dry land made up mostly of sand (desert)

DISCUSSION QUESTIONS

1   What did the grandmother (The Old One) mean when she said she would go to Mother Earth? (She was going to die.) How do you think she knew she was going to Mother Earth? (Annie's mother said the Old Ones knew. Children's individual answers may vary.)

2   Why did Annie's mother and grandmother weave rugs and blankets? (Answers may vary but might include to use and to sell.) Does anyone in your family do things similar to weaving, i.e., knitting, crocheting, embroidery, etc. If so, what? (Answers may vary.)

3   How is Annie's life different from yours? (Answers may vary.) How is Annie's life similar to yours? (Answers may vary.)

4   What are some of the things Annie did to slow down her mother's weaving? (She misbehaved in school, turned the sheep loose, pulled the threads of yarn from the woven rug) How do you think Annie felt about doing these things? (Answers may vary.)

5   Would you like to be Annie's neighbor? Why or why not? (Answers may vary.)

6   Grandmother asked Annie and Annie's mother and father what they would like of hers. What did each one take? (Annie—weaving stick, Annie's mother—the rug, Annie's father—silver belt) Do you think these were good choices for each of them? Why or why not? (Answers may vary.)

7   What do you think happened to the Old One (the grandmother) at the end of the story? Explain. (Answers may vary.)

8   Why did Annie finally decide it was time to learn to weave? (Answers may vary.)

Bulletin Board
Put the caption "Things We've Learned to Do" on the chalkboard. Distribute the form below and ask the children to complete it. Place their work on the bulletin board.

Name _____ Date _____

ACTIVITY SHEET 1

Directions
In the story *Annie and the Old One*, Annie learned how to weave. Think of something you have learned to do and the complete the following:

What did you learn? _____

_____

How did you learn to do it? _____

_____

When did you learn to do it? _____

_____

Make an illustration below to show what you learned to do.

From *Read It Again! Multicultural Books for the Primary Grades*, published by GoodYearBooks. Copyright © 1993 Liz Rothlein and Terri Christman Wild.

Name _____   Date _____

ACTIVITY SHEET 2

Directions
In the boxes, draw two things about the place where
Annie lived that are different from where you live. You
can get ideas from the story and the illustrations.

ANNIE AND
THE OLD ONE

ACTIVITY SHEET 3

Name _____ Date _____

Directions
Describe what you think are the saddest, bravest,
happiest, and best parts of *Annie and the Old One*.
Draw a picture that tells about each part you have
chosen.

The saddest part was ____

_____

_____

_____

The bravest part was ____

_____

_____

_____

The happiest part was ____

_____

_____

_____

The best part was ____

_____

_____

_____

From *Read It Again! Multicultural Books for the Primary Grades*, published by GoodYearBooks. Copyright © 1993 Liz Rothlein and Terri Christman Wild.

Name _____ Date _____

ACTIVITY SHEET 4

Directions
Below are things Annie does in the book *Annie and the Old One*. Read each statement and complete the questions below.

Annie helped watch the sheep.
Annie carried pails of water to the cornfield.
Annie walked to the bus stop and waited on the yellow bus.
Annie lived in a hogan.
Annie sat at her grandmother's feet and listened to stories.
Annie watched her mother weave.
Annie helped her grandmother gather twigs and brush.
Annie went to school.
Annie helped cook.
Annie learned to weave.

What two things from Annie's list would you like to do?

1. _____

Explain _____

2. _____

Explain _____

What two things from Annie's list would you *not* like to do?

1. _____

Explain _____

2. _____

Explain _____

What are two things that Annie does that are similar to what you do?

1. _____

Explain _____

2. _____

Explain _____

ADDITIONAL ACTIVITIES

1 Show children the picture of Annie's hogan on page 3 of the book. Then provide clay, sticks, bark, cardboard, glue, yarn, etc. Ask children to work in groups to make a replica of Annie's hogan.

2 Obtain a copy of *Book of American Indian Games* by Allen A.Macfarlan (Association Press, 1958). Help children learn some of the Indian games found in this book.

3 Create a weaving activity by introducing paper weaving. Begin by folding a piece of colored construction paper in half lengthwise. Then cut strips approximately one inch wide along the folded side without going all the way to the ends of the paper. From another color of paper, cut fairly narrow strips (approximately 3/4 inch wide) which will be woven into the first sheet of paper. Help children learn how to weave the individual narrow strips through the paper that has the strips. For more realistic weaving, looms can be made from a picture frame or wood rectangle. Wrap with warp threads (threads going up and down). Then use a needle or a stick as a shuttle and a ruler to separate the warp threads as the children weave yarn/thread through the warp threads.

4 The fourth Friday in September is celebrated in many states and communities as American Indian Day. For information on resources to help students learn more about Indian culture, write to Canyon Records, 4143 North 16th Street, Phoenix, AZ 85016, and ask for a catolog of records, cassettes, posters, slides, and other materials that relate to Native Americans. Use them in helping students plan an American Indian Day.

5 Read books such as *Warrior of the Sioux* by Jane Fleischer (Troll Associates, 1979) and *The Spider, the Cave, and the Pottery Bowl* by Eleanor Clymer (Hopi) (Dell, 1989), which introduce different Indian tribes. Help the children compare and contrast these books with *Annie and the Old One*. Talk about characters, setting, how the stories begin and end, etc. Ask the children which story they like best and why.

6 Annie liked to listen to stories her grandmother told. Invite grandparents to come in and tell their stories to the children.

BIG THUNDER MAGIC

Author
Craig Kee Strete

Illustrator
Craig Brown

Publisher
Greenwillow Books, 1990

Pages	**Interest Level**
29	Gr. K-4

Reading Level
Gr. 3

Other Books by Strete
The Bleeding Man and Other Science Fiction Stories; Paint Your Face on a Drowning in the River; When Grandfather Journeys into Winter

Summary
This is a story about Thunderspirit, a very small, timid ghost, and his friend, Nanabee the sheep. Nanabee lives with the Great Chief in a Pueblo, and Thunderspirit likes to sleep next to Nanabee at night. One day the Great Chief and Nanabee go to city, and Thunderspirit follows them. While in a park, Nanabee is captured and taken to a zoo. Using his magic powers, Thunderspirit rescues Nanabee, and they return to the Pueblo with the Great Chief.

Introduction
Read the title of the book *Big Thunder Magic*, and show the children the cover of the book. Then ask them to predict what the "big thunder magic" is. Write their predictions on the chalkboard. After reading the story, discuss what the "big thunder magic" was actually about.

Key Vocabulary
After children have heard the story, write these words on the chalkboard and choral read. Then discuss the meaning of each word and use it in the context of a phrase or sentence.

pueblo	medicine	magic	ghost
desert	lightning	thunder	chief

Key Vocabulary Instruction
Give each student a copy of the the worksheet on page 106. Ask the children to look at the words written correctly as they unscramble the words on the worksheet. Tell them to write the word correctly on the blank next to the scrambled word.

Name _____ Date _____

Directions
Unscramble the words below, writing them on the blank
lines.

1. tseerd _____

2. lbopeu _____

3. rtuhnde _____

4. acgmi _____

5. tgosh _____

6. cfihe _____

7. glniihntg _____

8. nemecdii _____

From *Read It Again! Multicultural Books for the Primary Grades*, published by GoodYearBooks. Copyright © 1993 Liz Rothlein and Terri Christman Wild.

BIG THUNDER
MAGIC

DISCUSSION QUESTIONS

1 Where do Nanabee and Thunderspirit live? (A quiet pueblo at the edge of the desert) Describe what it looks like. (Answers may vary.)

2 Tell me about Thunderspirit. (Answers may vary.) What does he look like? What kind of a character is he, good or bad? (Answers may vary.)

3 Do you think the Great Chief knew about Thunderspirit? (Answers may vary.) Why or why not? (Answers may vary.)

4 Was it a good idea for the Great Chief to take Nanabee the sheep with him to the city? (Answers may vary.) Why or why not? (Answers may vary.)

5 Where did Thunderspirit like to sleep? (Next to Nanabee.) Why? (Answers may vary, but might include: Because he kept him warm.)

6 Do you think Nanabee knew about Thunderspirit and could see him? (Answers may vary.) Why or why not? (Answers may vary.)

7 The Great Chief couldn't remember why he had gone to the city. Why do you think he went to the city? (Answers may vary.)

8 Did the Great Chief know that Nanabee was taken to the zoo? (Answers may vary.) Why or why not? What do you think would have happened to Nanabee if Thunderspirit hadn't performed his magic to get him out of the zoo? (Answers may vary.)

Bulletin Board
Tell students to pretend they have a friend like Thunderspirit. On the sheep pattern provided, ask the students to write what magic they'd want him to do for them. Label the bulletin board "Big Thunder Magic," and then adhere the children's lists to it.

Name _____ Date _____

Directions

In each box below, draw one thing about the place where Nanabee and Thunderspirit lived that is different from where you live. You can get ideas from the story and its pictures.

From *Read It Again! Multicultural Books for the Primary Grades*, published by GoodYearBooks. Copyright © 1993 Liz Rothlein and Terri Christman Wild.

Name _____ Date _____

Directions
There are many compound words in *Big Thunder Magic* that name people. A compound word is one that is made when two words are put together. Using the words below, put two words together to make a compound word. Write the compound word on the line provided.

dog & catcher = _____

Thunder & spirit = _____

paper & girl = _____

zoo & keeper = _____

milk & man = _____

Directions
Use the compound words from above to complete the following sentences.

1. A _____ saw Nanabee first.

2. The _____ said, "I only catch dogs."

3. A _____ delivers milk.

4. The _____ thought Nanabee was unusual.

5. _____ used magic from his medicine bag.

Write other compound words that you know.

_____

_____

_____

Name _____ Date _____

Directions
Thunderspirit created magic out of his medicine bag.
Imagine that you are writing your own book about a
magical character and answer the questions below.

1. Who would that character be? _____

_____

2. What would you name the character? _____

3. What would your character need to make magic? _____

_____

4. Where would your character live? _____

_____

5. Who would come to your character for magic? Why? _____

_____

6. Describe the magic that your character could do. _____

_____

Draw your magical character.

From *Read It Again! Multicultural Books for the Primary Grades*, published by GoodYearBooks. Copyright © 1993 Liz Rothlein and Terri Christman Wild.

ADDITIONAL ACTIVITIES

1 Discuss with the children that some of the events in the story could not actually happen, that they are make-believe. However, some of the events could happen; they are real. On the chalkboard, write "make-believe" at the top of one column and "real" at the top of another column. Then ask the children to tell you events in the story and decide in which column they belong. Write the events in the appropriate column.

2 In the story *Big Thunder Magic*, Thunderspirit and Nanabee lived in a pueblo. Obtain a copy of *Where Indians Live: American Indian Houses* by Nashone (Sierra Oaks Publishing Company, 1989). This is an excellent reference book for primary children that tells how Native Americans lived in the past as well as today. Another book, *The Pueblo* by Charlotte and David Yue (Houghton Mifflin, 1986) is a good adult reference that provides excellent illustrations and information about the Pueblo Indian homes. Allow time for the children to look through these and similar books. Then discuss what Thunderspirit's and Nanabee's lives were like living in a pueblo.

3 Discuss with children why Nanabee could not stay in the hotel with Great Chief. Put the children in pairs or small groups and ask them to list other places where Great Chief may want to go that Nanabee would not be allowed to go. Tell them to make a list of these places. Ask the pairs or groups of children to also think about where in the city Great Chief might have taken Nanabee instead of the park. Ask them to list these places also.

4 Thunderspirit made his ghost sounds but nobody could hear them above the city noises. On the chalkboard, do a webbing of city noises and country noises. For example:

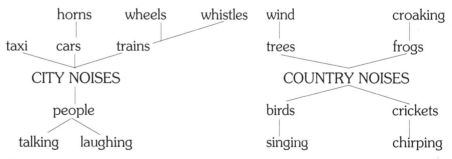

When the webs are complete, discuss which sounds the children prefer and why.

5 Discuss with the children that Thunderspirit's noises made the Great Chief happy and helped him sleep peacefully. Ask children to share what they like to do at bedtime to help them sleep peacefully.

THE LEGEND OF THE INDIAN PAINTBRUSH

Author
Tomie de Paola

Illustrator
Tomie de Paola

Publisher
G. P. Putnam's Sons, 1988

Pages	Interest Level
36	Gr. K-3

Reading Level
Gr. 2

Other Books by de Paola
Strega Nona; *The Legend of Bluebonnet*; *Cloud Book*; *Nana Upstairs and Nana Downstairs*; *Pancakes for Breakfast*; *The Popcorn Book*; *Andy: That's My Name*; *Bill and Pete*; *Charlie Needs a Cloak*; plus many other books.

Summary

In this retelling of an Indian tale, we learn how the plant now known as the Indian Paintbrush got its name. Little Gopher traveled across the plains with his people. He was an artist, but try as he might, he could not create the painting revealed to him in his Dream-Vision—one as pure as the colors of the evening sky. At last, his faithfulness and his artistry are rewarded. His legacy is this hearty plant whose flowers are as colorful as the setting sun.

Introduction

Have you ever dreamed about what you might do when you get older? Tell us about your dream. Have you thought about how you might make this dream a reality? Would you have to study? What and where? Would you need to practice? How? In the story we are about to read, you will learn about a young Indian boy who had a Dream-Vision that told him he would be an artist. His Dream-Vision became a reality.

Key Vocabulary

After children have heard the story, write these words on the chalkboard and choral read. Then discuss the meaning of each word and use it in the context of a phrase or sentence.

teepee	vision	warrior	custom
tribe	fade	struggle	deed

Key Vocabulary Instruction

Ask students to complete the worksheet on page 113.

From *Read It Again! Multicultural Books for the Primary Grades*, published by GoodYearBooks. Copyright © 1993 Liz Rothlein and Terri Christman Wild.

**ACTIVITY
WORKSHEET**

Name _____ Date _____

Directions
Use the vocabulary words to complete the following sentences:

teepee	vision	warrior	custom
tribe	fade	struggle	deed

1. I did a good _____ .

2. He was a strong _____ .

3. Would you like to live in a _____ ?

4. It is a _____ of the Indians to do that.

5. I had a _____ or dream about it.

6. The flower will _____ in color.

7. What _____ did she belong to?

8. The two argued and had a _____ .

DISCUSSION QUESTIONS

1 What was bothering Little Gopher? (Answers may vary, but should include—he was smaller than the rest of the children, he couldn't keep up with the others, etc.)

2 What did Little Gopher like to do when he was young? (He made toy warriors from scraps of leather and pieces of wood; he decorated smooth stones with the red juices from berries.)

3 What did he paint pictures of? (He painted pictures of great hunts, great deeds, Dream-Visions, and the sunset.)

4 Why did Little Gopher's pure white buckskin remain empty? (He couldn't find the colors of the sunset to use in painting on it.)

5 Why did Little Gopher finally get the colors he needed? (He was faithful to the people and true to his gift.)

6 How is Little Gopher's way of living different from yours? (Answers may vary.)

7 Do artists today use the same kinds of art supplies as Little Gopher? How are they alike? How are they different? (Answers may vary.)

8 Do you dream? If so, what are your dreams about? (Answers may vary.)

Bulletin Board

Create a bulletin board that is an extension of your introductory discussion. Remind children of your talk together about the dreams they have of what they would like to be when they are older. Ask them to illustrate their dreams. (Distribute 8 1/2" x 11" sheets of drawing paper.) Just as Little Gopher's name changed, ask them to write a new name for themselves under their pictures (He-Who-_____ or She-Who-_____). Place the pictures on a bulletin board entitled "Our Dream-Visions."

From *Read It Again! Multicultural Books for the Primary Grades*, published by GoodYearBooks. Copyright © 1993 Liz Rothlein and Terri Christman Wild.

THE LEGEND OF THE INDIAN PAINTBRUSH

ACTIVITY SHEET 1

Name _____   Date _____

Directions
On the buckskin below, draw and color a great deed you have done. Then, answer the questions about your greatest deed.

My Greatest Deed

Who were you with? _____

Where were you? _____

What did you do? _____

When did you do it? _____

Name _____ Date _____

Directions
A fact is something that can be proven as true. An opinion is something that cannot be proven true. Read each sentence below. Put an "F" in the blank if the statement is a fact. Place an "O" in the blank if the statement is an opinion.

_____ 1. Little Gopher made brushes from the hairs of different animals.

_____ 2. Little Gopher was a good painter.

_____ 3. Little Gopher painted on the skins of animals.

_____ 4. His paints were made out of crushed berries, flowers, and rocks of different colors.

_____ 5. Little Gopher's mother and father worried about him.

_____ 6. Little Gopher had enough brushes to paint his pictures.

_____ 7. His paints were just as good as the ones we have today.

_____ 8. Everyone liked Little Gopher's paintings.

_____ 9. Little Gopher found the colors of the sunset.

_____ 10. At the end of the story Little Gopher was called He-Who-Brought-the-Sunset-to-the-Earth.

Write one "fact" sentence.

_____

_____

Write one "opinion" sentence.

_____

_____

From *Read It Again! Multicultural Books for the Primary Grades*, published by GoodYearBooks. Copyright © 1993 Liz Rothlein and Terri Christman Wild.

THE LEGEND OF
THE INDIAN
PAINTBRUSH

Name _____ Date _____

ACTIVITY SHEET 3

Directions
Create your own legend. Pick a question below and write
your own story that answers it. Illustrate your legend on
the back of this page.

1. Why does the sun come up in the east and set in the west?

2. Why are there four seasons?

3. Why do we have mountains?

4. Why are there stars in the sky at night?

5. Why are the oceans so big and deep?

The Legend of _____

told by _____

_____

_____

_____

_____

_____

_____

_____

_____

_____

ADDITIONAL ACTIVITIES

1 Tomie de Paola also wrote *The Legend of the Bluebonnet: An Old Tale of Texas*. Read this story aloud to the students. Discuss how the legends are alike and how they are different. Discuss which story they liked best and why.

2 Using an encyclopedia, read about the Indian Paintbrush to the students. Then, give each student a large sheet of white drawing paper. Have them use crayons or paints to create a hill full of Indian Paintbrushes. Encourage them to use the colors of the sunset—reds, yellows, and oranges.

3 At the end of this story, Little Gopher's name was changed to He-Who-Brought-the-Sunset-to-the-Earth. Have students list their family members' names on a sheet of writing paper. Ask them to think of new names for each member of their family. For example, He-Who-Laughs-Often or She-Who-Cooks-So-Well.

4 Little Gopher decorated smooth stones with red juices from berries. Obtain some smooth stones or ask the children to bring some smooth stones to school. Get some berries such as strawberries, blueberries, or raspberries. Allow the children to mash the berries and then use the juice to decorate their stones. If berries are not available, use tempera paints.

5 Read (or summarize if it is more appropriate) and discuss the Author's Note at the end of the book with the children. Point out that the Indian Paintbrush is the state flower of Wyoming. Help children find out what the state flower is for your state. Then either show them the flower itself or a picture of it. Ask if any of them has seen this flower. Where? Finally, provide the children with large sheets of paper and ask them to draw and color a picture of their state flower.

6 Use the bibliography on pages 132 to 134 of this book to help you locate other tales from Native American folklore and share them with children. As you read, use a map of North America to show them where the people who first told these tales once lived.

From *Read It Again! Multicultural Books for the Primary Grades*, published by GoodYearBooks. Copyright © 1993 Liz Rothlein and Terri Christman Wild.

APPENDIX

VOCABULARY WORDS

The following words are key vocabulary words that are introduced and reinforced throughout this book.

adventure
argued
blinking
box
brocades
bucket
buildings
cakewalk
chief
claimed
continued
country
coyote
curandera
custom
daughter
deed
demanded
desert
dipper
director
disappeared
docked
downtown
embroidered
entered
factories
fade
flock
fortune-teller
fragrant
garden

ghost
glared
harbor
hogan
hoisting
honor
invisible
journey
kerosene
knocked
lamp
lifeguard
lightning
listened
loom
lowly
magic
magical
marvel
medicine
member
mesa
mesquite
Mexico
mountain
Navajo
nopal cactus
obeyed
outhouse
porch
possession
prepared

pueblo
queen
scrambling
servant
shark
shouting
shuttle
stable
station
stonecutter
struggle
tamales
teepee
threatened
thunder
tortillas
tracking
transformed
tribe
tutors
twice
village
vision
warp
warrior
washstand
wealth
weave
whispered
widow
worthy
woven

From *Read It Again! Multicultural Books for the Primary Grades*, published by GoodYearBooks. Copyright © 1993 Liz Rothlein and Terri Christman Wild.

The Stonecutter

ACTIVITY SHEET 2

1

2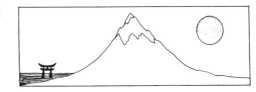

3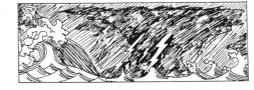

4

The Weaving of a Dream

ACTIVITY SHEET 2

1. could happen
2. couldn't happen
3. could happen
4. couldn't happen

5. could happen
6. couldn't happen
7. couldn't happen
8. could happen

Bigmama's

ACTIVITY SHEET 2

1. The family was riding on a train.
2. The family drove with Uncle Slank on a dirt road.
3. Bigmama and Bigpapa were waiting on the porch.
4. The children took off their shoes and socks.
5. The children dropped a bucket into the well to get water to drink.
6. The children went fishing.

Mufaro's Beautiful Daughter

ACTIVITY SHEET 1

ACTIVITY SHEET 2

<u>5</u> square   <u>3</u> little

<u>1</u> sad   <u>4</u> light

<u>8</u> boy   <u>7</u> ugly

<u>6</u> short   <u>2</u> hot

Big Thunder Magic

VOCABULARY WORKSHEET

1. desert
2. pueblo
3. thunder
4. magic
5. ghost
6. chief
7. lightning
8. medicine

From *Read It Again! Multicultural Books for the Primary Grades*, published by GoodYearBooks. Copyright © 1993 Liz Rothlein and Terri Christman Wild.

ACTIVITY SHEET 2

1. dogcatcher

2. Thunderspirit

3. papergirl

4. zookeeper

5. milkman

The Legend of the Indian Paintbrush

VOCABULARY WORKSHEET

1. deed
2. warrior
3. teepee
4. custom
5. vision
6. fade
7. tribe
8. struggle

ACTIVITY SHEET 2

1. F	6. O
2. O	7. O
3. F	8. O
4. F	9. F
5. F	10. F

RESOURCES

General Multicultural Literature

Baer, E. (1990). *This is the way we go to school: A book about children around the world.* New York: Scholastic.

Brisson, P. (1991). *Magic carpet.* New York: Bradbury.

Dorros, A. (1992). *This is my house.* New York: Scholastic.

Feeney, S. (1985). *Hawaii is a rainbow.* Honolulu: The University of Hawaii Press.

Hoffman, P. (1991). *Meatball.* New York: HarperCollins.

Isadora, R. (1983). *City seen from A to Z.* New York: Greenwillow Books.

Kelly, E. (1984). *Happy New Year.* Minneapolis, MN: Carolrhoda Books.

Kindergarten of Cheltenham Elementary School. (1991). *We are all alike. We are all different.* New York: Scholastic.

Krupp, R. R. (1992). *Let's go traveling.* New York: Morrow.

McPherson, J. (1992). *Chasing games from around the world.* Austin, TX: Steck-Vaughn.

Moll, P. B. (1991). *Children and books I: African American story books and activities for all children.* Tampa, FL: Hampton Mae Institute.

Morris, A. (1989). *Bread, bread, bread.* New York: Lothrop, Lee & Shepard.

Morris, A. (1990). *On the go.* New York: Lothrop, Lee & Shepard.

Sage, J. (1991). *The little band.* New York: Macmillan.

Shannon, G. (1991). *More stories to solve: Fifteen folktales from around the world.* New York: Greenwillow Books.

Showers, P. (1985). *Your skin and mine.* New York: Harper & Row.

Sierra, J. (1988). *The Oryx multicultural folktale series: Cinderella.* Phoenix, AZ: Oryx.

Sierra, J. & Kaminski, R. (1991). *Multicultural stories to tell young children.* Phoenix, AZ: Oryx.

Simon, N. (1976). *Why am I different?* Chicago: Albert Whitman.

Warren, J. & McKinnon, E. (1988). *Small world celebrations: multicultural holidays to celebrate with young children.* Everett, WA: Warren Publishing House.

Related Literature About the People, Traditions, and Folklore of Asia

Adams, E. B. (ed.) (1982). *Korean Cinderella.* Seoul, Korea: Seoul International Publishing House.

Adams, E. B. (1981). *Blindman's daughter.* Seoul International Publishing House.

Bang, M. (1987). *The paper crane.* New York: Morrow.

Battles, E. (1978). *What does the rooster say, Yoshio?.* Chicago: Albert Whitman.

Bedard, M. (1992). *The nightingale.* New York: Clarion.

Brown, T. (1987). *Chinese New Year.* New York: Henry Holt.

Chang, K. (1977). *The iron moonhunter.* San Francisco: Children's Book Press.

Cheng, H. (1976). *The Chinese New Year.* New York: Henry Holt.

Coblence, J-M. (1988). *Asian Civilizations.* New York: Silver Burdett.

Coutant, H. (1974). *First snow.* New York: Knopf.

Demi. (1990). *The magic boat.* New York: Henry Holt.

Dooley, N. (1991). *Everybody cooks rice.* Minneapolis, MN: Carolrhoda Books.

Fogel, J. (1979). *Wesley Paul: Marathon runner.* New York: Lippincott.

Haskins, J. (1989). *Count your way through Korea.* Minneapolis, MN: Carolrhoda Books.

Hong, L. T. (1990). *How the ox star fell from heaven.* Chicago: Albert Whitman.

Jacobsen, P., and Kristensen, P. (1986). *A family in Thailand.* The Bookwright Press.

Lee, J. M. (1987). *Ba Nam.* New York: Henry Holt.

Lye, K. (1985). *Take a trip to South Korea.* New York: Franklin Watts.

Mahy, M. (1990). *The seven Chinese brothers.* New York: Scholastic.

Martin, P. M. (1962). *The rice bowl pet.* New York: Crowell.

Mau-Chiu, C. (1965). *The little doctor.* Peking: Foreign Language Press.

Miller, M. (1989). *The moon dragon.* Illustrated by Ian Deuchar. New York: Dial.

Moffett, E. (1987). *Korean ways.* Seoul, Korea: Seoul International Publishing House.

Moon, G. (1960). *Moy moy.* New York: Scribner's.

Morimoto, J. (1988). *Mouse's marriage.* New York: Puffin.

Mosel, A. (1968). *Tikki Tikki Tembo.* New York: Holt Rinehart.

Pinkwater, M. (1975). *Wingman.* New York: Dodd, Mead.

Say, A. (1988). *A river dream.* Boston: Houghton Mifflin.

Say, A. (1989). *The lost lake.* Boston: Houghton Mifflin.

Say, A. (1990). *El Chino.* Boston: Houghton Mifflin.

Say, A. (1991). *Tree of cranes.* Boston: Houghton Mifflin.

Snyder, D. (1988). *The boy of the three-year nap.* Boston: Houghton Mifflin.

Surat, M. M. (1983). *Angel child, Dragon child.* Racine, WI: Raintree.

Thompson, R., and Thompson, N. (1988). *A family in Thailand.* Minneapolis, MN: Learner Publications.

Tran Khank Tuyet. (1987). *The little weaver of Thai-Yen village.* San Francisco: Children's Book Press.

Wallace, I. (1984). *Chin Chiang and the dragon's dance.* New York: Atheneum.

Yashima, M. & T. (1961). *Momo's kitten.* New York: Puffin.

Yashima, T. (1955). *Crow boy*. New York: Viking.

Yashima, T. (1958). *Umbrella*. New York: Viking.

Yi, Y., & Liang, K. (1966). *I am on duty today*. Peking: Foreign Language Press.

Yolen, J. (1989). *Hands*. Littleton, MA: Sundance.

Literature Related to the Traditions and Folklore of Africa and the African American Experience

Aardema, V. (1975). *Why mosquitoes buzz in people's ears: A West African tale*. New York: Dial.

Aardema, V. (1985). *Bimwili and Zimwi*. New York: Dial.

Aardema, V., reteller. (1991). *Traveling to Tondo: A tale of the Nkundo of Zaire*. New York: Alfred A. Knopf.

Adams, R. (1969). *Great Negroes, Past and present*. Chicago: Afro-Am Publishing Co.

Adoff, A. (1973). *Black is brown is tan*. New York: Harper & Row.

Adoff, A. (1974). *My black me: A beginning book of Black poetry*. New York: Dutton.

Alexander, M. (1969). *The story grandmother told*. New York: Dial.

Anderson, L. (1973). *The day the hurricane happened*. New York: Scribner's.

Baron, V. O. (1969). *Here I am!* New York: Dutton.

Blue, R. (1969). *Black, black, beautiful black*. New York: Franklin Watts.

Boone-Jones, M. (1967). *Martin Luther King, Jr.: A picture story*. Chicago: Childrens Press.

Bradman, T. (1988). *Wait and see*. New York: Oxford University Press.

Bryan, A. (1974). *Walk together children: Black American spirituals*. New York: Atheneum.

Bryan, A. (1980). *Beat the story-drum, pum-pum*. New York: Atheneum.

Bryan, A. (1991). *All night, all day: A child's first book of African-American sprituals*. New York: Atheneum.

Caines, J. (1980). *Window wishing*. New York: Harper & Row.

Cameron, A. (1987). *Julian's glorious summer*. New York: Random House.

Church, V. (1971). *Colors around me*. Chicago: Afro-Am Publishing Co.

Clifton, L. (1970). *Some of the days of Everett Anderson*. New York: Holt, Rinehart and Winston.

Clifton, L. (1973). *The boy who didn't believe in spring*. New York: Dutton.

Clifton, L. (1973). *Don't you remember?*. New York: Dutton.

Clifton, L. (1973). *Good, says Jerome*. New York: Dutton.

Clifton, L. (1974). *Everett Anderson's year*. New York: Holt, Rinehart and Winston.

Clifton, L. (1983). *Everett Anderson's Goodbye*. New York: Holt, Rinehart, and Winston.

Courlander, H. (1962). *The king's drum, and other African stories*. New York: Harcourt Brace Jovanovich.

Deasy, M. (1974). *City ABC's*. New York: Walker.

Dragonwagon, C. (1990). *Home place*. New York: Macmillan.

Ellis, V. F. (1990). *Afro-Bets first book about Africa*. Orange, NJ: Just Us Books.

Fassler, J. (1971). *Don't worry, dear*. New York: Human Sciences Press.

Feelings, M. (1970). *Zamani goes to market*. New York: Seabury Press.

Feelings, M. (1971). *Moja means one: A Swahili counting book*. New York: Dial.

Feelings, M. (1992). *Jambo means hello: Swahili alphabet book*. New York: Dial.

Gray, G. (1972). *A kite for Bennie*. New York: McGraw-Hill.

Gray, G. (1974). *Send Wendell*. New York: McGraw-Hill.

Greenberg, P. (1988). *Rosie and Roo*. Washington, DC: The Growth Program Press.

Greenfield, E. (1978). *Honey, I love: And other love poems*. New York: Harper & Row.

Greenfield, E. (1973). *Rosa Parks*. New York: Thomas Y. Crowell.

Greenfield, E. (1974). *She come bringing me that little baby girl*. Philadelphia: Lippincott.

Greenfield, E. (1977). *African dream*. New York: John Day Co.

Greenfield, E. (1984). *Me and Neesie*. New York: Thomas Y. Crowell.

Greenfield, E. (1988). *Grandpa's face*. New York: Philomel.

Grifalconi, A. (1990). *Osa's pride, Vol. 1*. Boston: Little, Brown.

Haley, G. (1970). *A story, a story*. New York: Atheneum.

Hamilton, V. (1985). *The people could fly: American black tales*. New York: Alfred A. Knopf.

Hamilton, V. (1989). *The bells of Christmas*. New York: Harcourt Brace Jovanovich.

Hayes, S. (1991). *Eat up, Gemma*. New York: Lothrop, Lee & Shepard.

Hill, E. S. (1991). *Evan's corner*. New York: Viking.

Hudson, C., & Ford, B. (1990). *Bright eyes, brown skin*. Orange, NJ: Just Us Books.

Isadora, R. (1991). *At the crossroads*. New York: Greenwillow Books.

Johnson, A. (1990). *Do like Kyla*. New York: Orchard.

Johnson, A. (1990). *When I am old with you*. New York: Orchard.

Jones, R. C. (1991). *Matthew and Tilly*. New York: Dutton.

Jordan, J. (1981). *Kimako's story*. New York: Houghton Mifflin.

King, Jr., M. L. (1991). *I have a dream*. Littleton, MA: Sundance.

Kirn, A. (1968). *Beeswax catches a thief*. New York: Norton.

Knutson, B. (1990). *How the guinea fowl got her spots: A Swahili tale of friendship*. Minneapolis, MN: Carolrhoda Books.

Lexau, J. M. (1970). *Benjie on his own*. New York: Dial.

Little, L. J., & Greenfield, E. (1978). *I can do it by myself*. New York: Thomas Y. Crowell.

McDermott, G., reteller. (1972). *Anansi the spider: A tale from Ashanti*. New York: Henry Holt.

McGovern, A. (1969). *Black is beautiful*. New York: Scholastic.

Mandelbaum, P. (1990). *You be me, I'll be you*. Brooklyn, NY: Kane-Miller.

Mattox, C. W., editor. (1990). *Shake it to the one that you love the best: Play songs and lullabies from black musical traditions*. El Sobrante, CA: Warren-Mattox.

Mendez, P. (1991). *The black snowman*. New York: Scholastic.

Mennen, I., & Daly, N. (1992). *Somewhere in Africa*. New York: Dutton.

Michels, B., & White, B. (1983). *Apples on a stick: The folklore of Black children*. New York: Coward-McCann.

Monjo, F. N. (1970). *The drinking gourd*. New York: Harper & Row.

Musgrove, M. W. (1976). *Ashanti to Zulu: African traditions*. New York: Dial.

Nolan, M. (1978). *My daddy don't go to work*. Minneapolis, MN: Carolrhoda Books.

Oliver, E. M. (1981). *Black Mother Goose book*. Brooklyn, NY: Gaus.

Rosenberg, M. B. (1986). *Living in two worlds*. New York: Lothrop, Lee & Shepard.

Steptoe, J. (1969). *Stevie*. New York: Harper & Row.

Steptoe, J. (1972). *Birthday*. New York: Holt, Rinehart and Winston.

Thomas, I. (1973). *Lordy, Aunt Hattie*. New York: Harper & Row.

Thomas, I. (1974). *Walk home tired, Billy Jenkins*. New York: Harper & Row.

Thomas, I. (1976). *My street's a morning cool street*. New York: Harper & Row.

Walter, M. (1986). *Justin and the best biscuits in the world*. New York: Lothrop, Lee & Shepard.

Welber, R. (1972). *The train*. New York: Pantheon.

Williams, K. L. (1990). *Galimoto*. New York: Lothrop, Lee & Shepard.

Williams, V. B. (1986). *Cherries and cherry pits.* New York: Greenwillow Books.

Wilson, B. P. (1990). *Jenny*. New York: Macmillan.

Yee, S., & Kokin, L. (1978). *Got me a story*. San Francisco: St. John's Educational Threshold Center.

Literature Related to Hispanic Cultures and the Hispanic American Experience

Acuna, R. (1971). *A Mexican American chronicle*. New York: American Books.

Ada, A. F. (1991). *The gold coin*. New York: Atheneum.

Adoff, A. (1988). *Flamboyan*. New York: Harcourt Brace Jovanovich.

Angeles. (1991). *Tortilla for Emillia*. Littleton, MA: Sundance.

Atkinson, M. (1979). *Maria Teresa*. Carrboro, NC: Lollipop Power.

Barry, R. (1971). *Ramon and the pirate gull*. New York: McGraw-Hill.

Blue, R. (1971). *I am here/Yo Estoy Aqui*. New York: Henry Holt.

Brown, T. (1985). *Hello, amigos!* New York: Holt, Rinehart, and Winston.

Brusca, M. C. (1991). *On the pampas*. New York: Holt, Rinehart, and Winston.
Clifton, L. (1976). *Everett Anderson's best friend*. New York: Henry Holt.

Delacre, L. (1989). *Arroz Con Leche: Popular songs and rhymes from Latin America*. New York: Scholastic.

Delacre, L. (1990). *Las Navidades: Popular Christmas songs from Latin America*. New York: Scholastic.

Ets, M. H. (1963). *Gilberto and the wind*. New York: Viking.

Fradin, D. (1981). *New Mexico: In words and pictures*. San Francisco: Children's Book Press.

Hewett, J. (1990). *Hector lives in the United States now: The Story of a Mexican-American child*. New York: J. B. Lippincott.

Hitte, K., & Hayes, W. (1970). *Mexicali soup*. New York: Parents Magazine Press.

Kouzel, D. (1977). *The cuckoo's reward/El Premio del Cuco*. New York: Doubleday.

Macmillan, D., & Freeman, D. (1986). *My best friend Martha Rodriquez: Meeting a Mexican-American family*. Englewood Cliffs, NJ: Julian Messner.

Martel, C. (1987). *Yagua days*. New York: Dial.

Maury, I. (1976). *My mother the mail carrier/Mi mama, la Cartera*. New York: Feminist Press.

Rosario, I. (1987). *Idalia's project ABC: An urban alphabet book in English and Spanish*. New York: Holt, Rinehart and Winston.

Sonneborn, R. (1987). *Friday night is papa night*. New York: Puffin.

Winter, J. & Winter, J. (1991). *Diego*. New York: Alfred A. Knopf.

Related Literature About Native Americans, Their Traditions and Folklore

Aliki. (1986). *Corn is maize: The gift of the Indian*. New York: Thomas Y. Crowell.

Baker, B. (1962). *Little runner of the longhouse*. New York: Harper & Row.

Baker, O. (1989). *Where the buffaloes begin*. New York: Viking.

Bales, C. A. (1972). *Kevin Cloud: Chippewa boy in the city*. Chicago: Reilly & Lee.

Baylor, B. (1976). *Hawk, I'm your brother*. New York: Macmillan.

Behrens, J. (1983). *Powwow: Festivals and holidays*. Chicago: Childrens Press.

Blood, C., & Link, M. (1976). *The goat in the rug*. New York: Four Winds Press.

Brenner, B. (1978). *Wagon wheels*. New York: Harper & Row.

Cameron, A. (1988). *Spider woman*. Madeira Park, BC: Harbour Publishers.

Carey, V. S. (1990). *Quail song: A Pueblo Indian tale*. New York: Holt.

Clark, A. N. (1991). *In my mother's house*. New York: Viking.

Clymer, E. (1989). *The spider, the cave and the pottery bowl*. New York: Dell.

Cohen, C. L., adaptor. (1988). *The mud pony: A traditional Skidi Pawnee tale*. New York: Scholastic.

Crowder, J., & Hill, F. (1969). *Stephanie and the coyote*. Bernalillow, NM: Upper Strata.

De Paola, T., reteller. (1983). *The legend of the Bluebonnet: An old tale of Texas*. New York: Putnam.

Fritz, J. (1982). *The good giants and the bad pukwudgies*. New York: Putnam.

Goble, P. (1978). *Award puzzles: The girl who loved wild horses*. New York: Bradbury.

Goble, P., reteller. (1988). *Iktomi and the boulder*. New York: Orchard.

Goble, P., reteller. (1990). *Iktomi and the ducks: A Plains Indian tale*. New York: Orchard.

Goble, P. (1991). *Crow chief*. New York: Orchard.

Goble, P., reteller. (1990). *Iktomi and the buffalo skull: A Plains Indian story*. New York: Orchard.

Grossman, V. (1991). *Ten little rabbits*. San Francisco: Chronicle.

Hoyt-Goldsmith, D. (1990). *Totem pole*. New York: Holiday House.

Lopez, A. (1991). *Celebration*. Littleton, MA: Sundance.

McDermott, G. (1974). *Arrow to the sun: A Pueblo Indian tale*. New York: Viking.

McDermott, G. (1991). *Flecha al Sol: Un Cuento de Los Indios Pueblo*. New York: Puffin.

Martin, B., Jr., & Archambault, J. (1987). *Knots on a counting rope*. New York: Holt, Rinehart, and Winston.

Moon, G. (1967). *One little Indian*. Chicago: Albert Whitman.

New Mexico People and Energy Collective Staff, et al. (1981). *Red ribbons for Emma*. Berkeley, CA: New Seed Press.

Red Hawk, R. (1988). *A, B, C's the American Indian way*. New Castle, CA: Sierra Oaks.

From *Read It Again! Multicultural Books for the Primary Grades*, published by GoodYearBooks. Copyright © 1993 Liz Rothlein and Terri Christman Wild.

READ IT AGAIN! MULTICULTURAL 133

Rodanas, K. (1992). *Dragonfly's tale*. New York: Clarion.

Shor, P. (1973). *When the corn is red*. New York: Abingdon.

Sleator, W. (1970). *The angry moon*. Boston: Little, Brown.

Steltzer, U. (1984). *A Haida potlatch*. Seattle, WA: University of Washington Press.

Steptoe, J. (1989). *The story of jumping mouse: A Native American legend*. New York: Morrow.

United Indians of All Tribes. (1980). *Sharing our worlds: Native American children today*. Seattle, WA: Author.

Waterton, B. (1991). *A salmon for Simon*. Columbia, SC: Camden House.

Wondriska, W. (1972). *The stop*. New York: Holt, Rinehart and Winston.

Teacher Resources

Afro-Am Education Materials, 819 S. Wabash Ave., Chicago, IL 60605. (312) 922-1147. Catalog of books, records, dolls, posters, puzzles, and skin-colored crayons.

American Indian Resource Center, Huntington Park Library, 6518 Miles Ave., Huntington Park, CA 90255. (213) 583-1461. Books and curriculum ideas for the study of Native Americans.

Anti-Bias Curriculum: Tools for Empowering Young Children, National Association for the Education of Young Children, 1834 Connecticut Avenue, N.W., Washington, DC 20009-5786. A practical book that shows adults how to stand up for what's right and how to empower children so they can too.

Bilingual Publications Co., 270 Lafayette Street, New York, NY 10012. (212) 431-3500. FAX (212) 431-3567. Books in Spanish for all ages, from children to adults. The primary sources for the books are Mexico, Latin America, and the Caribbean. The collection ranges from children's books to adult non-fiction, especially self-help, parenting, health and nutrition, and fiction from Latin America. Fully annotated catalogues are also available, and books in special areas of interest can be found.

Council on Interracial Books for Children, P. O. Box 1263, New York, NY 10023. (212) 757-5339. Resources to counter bias in school and society are developed and produced here. Audiovisual materials such as filmstrips and videos, as well as lesson plans and books are available for both children and adults.

From *Read It Again! Multicultural Books for the Primary Grades,* published by GoodYearBooks. Copyright © 1993 Liz Rothlein and Terri Christman Wild.

Education Development Center, Inc., 55 Chapel Street, Newton, MA 02160. (617) 969-7100. Source of "We are family," a black-and-white poster displaying a collection of 32 photographs of a variety of families (multiracial and multigenerational). This is also the location of the Women's Educational Equity Act Publishing Center, which has curriculum and teacher in-service materials about sex inequities in education.

Global Village Toys, 2210 Wilshire Blvd., Suite 262, Santa Monica, CA 90403. (213) 459-5188. Source of excellent early childhood books and materials for implementing anti-bias curriculum.

Japanese American Curriculum Project, 414 Third St., San Mateo, CA 94401. (415) 343-9408. Source of Japanese-American and other Asian-American curriculum materials.

Lakeshore Curriculum Materials, 2695 E. Domingues St., Carson, CA 90749. (213) 537-8600. Source of multicultural materials including dolls of both sexes and in contemporary dress representing Native American, Asian, Hispanic, and African-American cultures, excellent puzzles.

Liberation Bookstore, 421 Lenox Ave., New York, NY 10037. (212) 281-4615. Source of both adult and children's books about African-Americans.

Museum of the American Indian, Broadway at 155 Street, New York, NY 10032. Ask for information on slides, books, and a catalog.
The National Clearinghouse for Bilingual Education, George Washington University, 1118 22nd Street, N.W., Washington, DC 20037. Send your name and address and 50 cents to receive copies of "Helping Your Child Use the Library." Available in Spanish ("Como ayudar a sus hijos a usar la biblioteca") and English.

Native American Educational Program, P.S. 199, West 107 Street, New York, NY 10025. Information about posters and records is available.

Navajo Curriculum Center Press, Rough Rock Demonstration School, P.O. Box 217, Chinle, AZ 86503. (602) 728-3311. This is a wonderful source for materials on Navajo culture.

Office for Civil Rights, Office for Special Concerns, U.S. Department of Education, 330 C St. S.W., Washington, DC 20202. (202) 732-1213. Source of materials about civil rights.

Puerto Rican Resource Units, State Education Department, Bureau of Bilingual Education, Albany, NY12234. (518) 474-2121. Source of curriculum materials and comprehensive bibliography.

Raintree Steck-Vaughn Library, 310 W. Wisconsin Avenue, Milwaukee, WI 53203. (800) 558-7264. Publishers of a collection of 24 multicultural books with tapes for ages 7-12 entitled, "Children's Book Press."

Start-Up Multiculturalism, Pembroke Publishers. P.O. Box 1192, Lewiston, NY 14092. (416) 477-0650. Source of activities to help students explore their cultural roots. blackline masters and an annotated bibliography of more than 200 classroom resources in fiction, non-fiction, games, videos, etc.

Steck-Vaughn Company, P.O. Box 26015, Austin, TX 78755. (800) 531-5015. Publishers of "My World Big Books," studies about different countries for grades 1-3.

Syracuse Cultural Workers, Box 6367, Syracuse, NY 13217. (315) 474-1132. Source of cards, posters, and pictures with various social and political messages, such as anti-racism. Catalogue.

United Indians of All Tribes Foundation, P.O. Box 99100, Seattle, WA 98199. (206) 285-4425. Source of curriculum and books about Northwest and Alaskan Native Americans.